CINEMATIC IDENTITY

CINEMATIC IDENTITY

ANATOMY OF A PROBLEM FILM

Cindy Patton

University of Minnesota Press
Minneapolis
London

THEORY OUT OF BOUNDS

Edited by Sandra Buckley, Michael Hardt, and Brian Massumi

Volume 29

Earlier versions of sections of chapter 3 previously appeared as "White Racism/Black Signs: Censorship and Images of Race Relations," *Journal of Communication Studies* 45, no. 2 (1995): 65–77; and an earlier version of portions of chapter 2 appeared as "To Die For," in *Novel Gazing: Queer Readings in Fiction,* ed. Eve Kosofsky Sedgwick (Durham, N.C.: Duke University Press, 1997), 330–52. We gratefully acknowledge Blackwell Synergy, which owns the *Journal of Communication Studies,* and Duke University Press for granting permission for these materials to appear here.

Published by the University of Minnesota Press
111 Third Avenue South, Suite 290
Minneapolis, MN 55401-2520
http://www.upress.umn.edu

Library of Congress Cataloging-in-Publication Data

Patton, Cindy, 1956–
    Cinematic identity : anatomy of a problem film / Cindy Patton.
        p. cm. — (Theory out of bounds ; 29)
    Includes bibliographical references and index.
    ISBN-13: 978-0-8166-3411-8 (hc : alk. paper)
    ISBN-10: 0-8166-3411-4 (hc : alk. paper)
    ISBN-13: 978-0-8166-3412-5 (pb : alk. paper)
    ISBN-10: 0-8166-3412-2 (pb : alk. paper)
    1. Social problems in motion pictures.   2. Minorities in motion
pictures.   3. Motion pictures—United States.   I. Title.
    PN1995.9.S62P38 2007
    791.43'65560973—dc22

                                                                    2007030262

Printed in the United States of America on acid-free paper

The University of Minnesota is an equal-opportunity educator
and employer.

12 11 10 09 08 07   10 9 8 7 6 5 4 3 2 1

CONTENTS

ACKNOWLEDGMENTS   vii

1. **American Celluloid: New Medium, New Citizen**   1
   Back to the Movies   1
   Race and Sexuality: Some Analytic Caveats   12
   Acting the Citizen   18

2. **In the Hearts of Men**   21
   To Die For   25
   Popularizing "the Problem": Politics as Melodrama   31
   Into the Closet   37
   Alienating Queer   43

3. **Censorship and the Problem Films**   47
   Censoring Race   47
   Cinematic Prohibition   53
   Race Mixing   56
   From Image to Story   59
   When a Kiss Is Not a Kiss   65
   Censoring Pinky   67

"Prejudice" and Epithet   71
The Dominoes Fall   75
Sacrilege and Race versus Sexuality   79

4. **Acting Up: The Performing American**   **81**
Signs of Apartheid   81
Acting History/The Historicity of Acting   84
Sound, Class, and Narrative   90
Narrative Sublation: Recalling-Forgetting History   99
The Question of Acting   101

5. **Two Conversations:**
   Black and White Americans on Film   **107**
Reading (in) "White Time":
   Black Performance and the Demand for Literacy   107
The Victim-Witness Story   112
Distinguishing Wrongs   115
An Ear for the Master's Tropes   119
"White Time"/Black Place   126
A Final Word, a Feeling, a Hope   136

APPENDIX. *PINKY:* A SYNOPSIS   139
NOTES   143
REFERENCES   173
FILMOGRAPHY   179
INDEX   182

ACKNOWLEDGMENTS

I owe many debts of gratitude for this very protracted project. Indeed, I sometimes feel that the "story of Pinky" traces my peripatetic academic career. I became interested in the film while I was working on my doctorate at the University of Massachusetts–Amherst in the late 1980s and would then have "read" the film psychoanalytically, as was the fashion of that day. This seemed somehow wrong, especially because of the very strong reactions the film provoked when I had the opportunity to screen it at Princeton, on invitation from Diana Fuss. The film read yet differently in Australia, where I worked on the project in the early 1990s during my four months at the Australian National University's Humanities Research Centre (thanks to John Ballard). That was when Sandi Buckley and Brian Massumi became series editors of Theory Out of Bounds and took an interest in the project. William Murphy at the University of Minnesota Press eventually took the book under contract; Richard Morrison later took over the project and was extraordinarily patient in continuing to support it as he moved up the ranks at that press. Dr. Calinda Lee assisted with the research while she was a doctoral student at Emory University, and she has published a fine essay on the reception of *Pinky* in the Black press at the time of the film's release. I owe the largest debt to Marguerite Pigeon, who now serves as the academic editor for my research unit at Simon Fraser University. Without her keen editorial eye and persistence, I might not have finished the project.

Finally, I want to note that my dog Alex departed in the fall of 2005. I do not know whether she had any lingering faith that this stack of papers would turn into a book, but I do know that I miss her and her ability to convince me from time to time that much of what humans do is rather silly.

AMERICAN CELLULOID
New Medium, New Citizen

Back to the Movies

Most people can tell you, admiringly or derisively, what paintings they like but they leave it to professional critics to make judgments about artistic value. In relation to movies,[1] however, no academic degree or special temperament is required: America's Academy Awards demonstrate nothing if not the superiority of consumer preference over critical acclaim. Everyone has an opinion about the movies.

The populist origins of American film once made movies an uncomfortable object for scholars from the traditional aesthetic fields: only sociologists and advertisers seemed to recognize that film did more than placate the culturally destitute classes. In the post–World War II period and accelerating through the 1970s, as the university was transformed by the increasing numbers of women, minority, and working-class scholars, film developed around itself an academic cottage industry.[2] Rather than striking out to find entirely new ways of studying movies, academic researchers stretched existing areas of literary studies, history, and, to a lesser extent, sociology to include it. Lodged in English departments, communications programs, and eventually in separate media and cultural studies programs, film theory often

Figure 1. *Postwar cinema's approach to America's "race" issues laid the ground-work for the visual paradigm used in later reportage of the civil rights movement. Performances like that of James Edwards, as the soldier in* Home of the Brave *(1949), prepared Americans to read the "Black presence" of leaders like Martin Luther King Jr.*

outstripped its object, while histories of film—part art form, part sociological experience—plodded along in the most conventional of styles. Trying to distinguish itself from earlier industry-driven market research, the sociology of film, especially the study of audiences, developed in several directions: questioning whether film violence makes people more violent, whether film promotes social values, and, in the past few decades, how people go about interpreting film.

American movies, and the celluloid medium itself, have thus been widely discussed as historical, social, and formal phenomenon. Nevertheless, the work on film adds up to something less than the sum of these parts. Historians are often unsystematic in their treatment of film *form,* while textual critics often ignore the historical significance of the films they deconstruct. Neither formalists nor historians have dealt well with audiences, especially audiences of the past. The missed opportunities that multimethod study might afford are especially noteworthy in the history of censorship; explanations of changing censorship practices largely ignore changes in film aesthetics and film interpretation. Reciprocally, academic critics have shown little formal interest in the censored films, and few audience analysts have considered the larger and different social effects of seeing—or not being allowed to see—a censored film.

In the extended meditation that follows, I experiment with and recombine means of conceptualizing and analyzing the place of film in American society, taking advantage of the well-worn paths when useful, but also coloring outside the lines when it seems something more ought to be said. Movies—or at least special movies whose significance I hope to justify—are perceptual spaces in which interpretive practices are enacted, modified, and carried over into nonfilmic social practices.[3] I am interested primarily in a change in one film technology—acting—and its principle medium, the actor's body. I contextualize this technology in a particular moment in the history of film acting, the emergence and depoliticization of the "problem film," circa 1947–59, in which, curiously enough, a style of acting becomes naturalized as "real." This style, a kind of watered-down version of the Method developed earlier for the stage, converges with the rise of a very American conceptualization of personal and social identity. This milquetoast humanism promotes tolerance, but understands tolerance to be the property of white, Christian males who use it to reestablish their position as the Universal from which are distinguished the particulars who need to be tolerated (Blacks, Jews, eventually women, other ethnic groups, the aged and disabled, and, arguably, gays and lesbians). For a few crucial years, the cinema became, I will contend here, a venue for working out the meaning and mode of representing authentic selfhood, a "look" and abstraction that are strikingly similar to the rediscovered "self" that was to emerge as a prerequisite for mobilizing the individual and her group in the context of post–World War II civil rights activism and discourse. I want to suggest that audiences watched and interpreted the film acting of the period in question through a set of socially shared visions of the world, and that these shifted to accommodate a new conception of how one could, to borrow from Goffman (1959, 1963), present the self in everyday life. In other words, audiences watched these films and co-evolved a new way of perceiving social identity and experiencing the "otherness" and yet universality of one another.

The period under study begins roughly in 1947 with the screening of *Gentleman's Agreement,* which inaugurates a somewhat ham-fisted experiment in modes of acting minority personhood. It ends with the 1959 Douglas Sirk–helmed version of *Imitation of Life,* the directorial and acting labors of which have long been praised, and which continues to be one of those films critics return to. The unfettered appreciation for the acting in *Imitation* suggests that by 1959 the Method-like style of acting that I will discuss in chapter 4 had been naturalized as the dominant dramatic film acting style. Equally importantly, this is the moment when the civil rights movement, long under way but transformed by World War II and by the shocking racism at the war's end,[4] was publicized as a phenomenon. Historians of social activism might balk at the suggestion that the acceptance of Method acting as the modality of "serious film" and the public discussion of the civil rights movement have something to do with each other. They might argue that, far from helping the plight of Black people, film mainly cast them in subordinate roles and served to enable white Americans to avoid fully coming to terms with the political dissent happening in their backyards.

But I want to propose that the "problem films," however superficially stereotypical in their presentation of race relations, also laid the groundwork for a shift in popular understandings of social identity that was essential to the subsequent feasibility of identity-based claims to civil redress. We might ponder what made it possible for Black actors like Sidney Poitier to become, almost overnight, "actors" rather than caricatures, and, equally, why White America seemed to change course over a mere few years to accept the civil rights movement as engaged in legitimate political speech. Both required the transformation of America's white viewing public from one heterogeneously responding to "the race problem" into one that shared a set of beliefs about the nature of Black experience and the source of racial hostility. The white public did not agree, of course, on the solution to the "race problem"; anti-Black violence, opposition to school desegregation, and contestation of Black voting rights all continued in one form or another. Nevertheless, a liberal frame was in place to understand and contain Black efforts, and this frame linked a sentimental and universalized Black experience of oppression with the legitimacy of civil rights.

But underneath the new liberal sentimentality toward racism there was a further division, a racial difference in how completely an individual could occupy the category "citizen." White self-consciousness was presumed to enable a kind of racial "passing," in which whites could partially grasp minority experience. But this, in effect, reduced minority experience to a particularity that could never achieve a universal—and therefore fully citizenlike—perspective. Black movements that contested identification with American liberalism and the American dream fell outside this frame and suffered for their efforts to propose alternative analyses of racism in America; the Black Panthers and other nationalists continued to carry the burden of white racist antipathy toward Black citizenship. But at least until the next refiguration of race, class, and American liberalism in the Reagan–Bush period—that is, at least until the rise of neo-liberalism—a particular understanding of Blackness exerted a gravitational pull on white Americans' liberal ideals.

One historical question that is, I suppose, unanswerable is how White America came so quickly to accept this representation of Black experience. Certainly, as my discussion of Ethel Waters (a major early- to mid-twentieth-century African American star) will reveal, there is a centuries-long cathexic relationship between whites' experience of their own brutality and Blacks' expression of pain. Jean-François Lyotard's work (1988/1983) suggests that such affectivity across the subjectivities of the violent and the violated may be products of modern systems of literature and law. I want to make a more specific and time-bound claim: that white Americans' capacity to "read" the 1950s–60s civil rights movement as taking part in legitimate political speech was contingent on their cultivation of a new affect, and this was accomplished not, as liberal historians would have it, by White America finding its conscience, but rather by way of a new semiotic regime, embodied through the wildly popular problem films that taught White America how to "connect" with its Other. These largely B-quality films stumble around in America's problems not through documentary exposition, but by introducing a new acting style into old genres. Several of the films that played this role in reeducating the White American sensibility were war movies.[5] Throughout the history of American cinema, war movies have been a vehicle for playing out myths of American plurality and, for that reason, they also offered a convenient format for playing with questions of how the dominant recognize the humanity of their other, and how the dominated "represent"—as rappers describe the rhetorical practices they use to indicate their locutionary space and time—their particularity and their experience. However, for reasons I will elaborate as we go along, the most important of the problem films—*Gentleman's Agreement* (1947) and *Pinky* (1949)—are melodramas whose audience was predominantly female at a historic apex of female consumerism, at the moment when consumption began most decisively to mark social identity, and at a time when U.S. governmentality defined *social* problems as domestic—even feminine—and *political* problems as public and masculine.

Although there are similarities in the acting of oppression in all the problem films, the Method-like style sits best (at least in hindsight) in the melodrama, and Method-like acting survived best in this genre.[6] As I will show in more detail in chapter 4, this shift in acting style within melodrama was not a benign mode for treating America's social problems. Rather the powerful change in social conceptions of identity and of affect, along with the acting shift it embodied, coincided with anticommunist efforts also centered on "understanding the other guy." As blunt an instrument as the House Committee on Un-American Activities (also known as HUAC) hearings became, they were only the most publicly distasteful of the post–World War II cultural and governmental efforts to reconstruct the meaning of social problems perceived to be at the root of the domestic attraction to communism. Although I emphasize *Pinky* and *Gentleman's Agreement* here, there are another dozen films and countless novels and magazine serials that are the intertexts in this national project of coming to grips with

American racism in the context of America's new role as world leader and plural people.

Pinky is arguably unique. It was a major box office success by a significant director (or rather two: John Ford gave up the project very late to Elia Kazan) and starred one of the best-known Black actresses of the 1940s (blues performer and stage actor Ethel Waters, who was nominated for an Academy Award for this role). *Pinky* was also censored (and the dispute went all the way to the Supreme Court). Remarkably enough, however, though *Pinky* is consistently mentioned, the film did not, until 2004 (see Courtney 2004; Petty 2004), merit even a single chapter in any book on racial stereotyping in films, in biographical or critical treatments of its director and cast, or in histories of film censorship. *Pinky* is rarely screened and was unavailable on videocassette when I began this project in the late 1980s.

As an enormously popular film about racial passing and racial identity, released on the cusp of the major legal innovations that were supposed to lead to racial integration, *Pinky* is visually accomplished and also historically significant. We can no longer undertake a conventional audience study, and I have declined to conduct oral histories of memories of the film, though such a project would be useful[7] in considering the significance of *Pinky*'s reception. I have chosen instead to analyze the movie reviews as a measure of the meaning and place of the film when it was released.

Work to uncover the racism in movies has resulted in a confusing body of material because a series of quite different concepts appear interchangeably to describe race-related prohibitions and their demise. For example, reviewers in the 1940s and 1950s, and film historians through the 1960s, referred to the collection of prohibitions as "the race bar," confusing specific prohibitions of images with the industry practice of discriminating against Black actors and film workers. The films themselves were described as dealing with "the Negro problem" and, later, as "problem" or "message" films. These terminological shifts and supplements are symptomatic of flaws in the larger attempt to conceptualize and confront racism without fully recalling the history of racist violence in America. Even when the idea of a "race bar" referred specifically to censorship practices, two related, but importantly different, ideas were conflated: "prejudice," which had been established as a concern through the censoring practices and legal opinions surrounding D. W. Griffith's *Birth of a Nation* (1915), and "miscegenation," which had been explicitly ruled out of bounds in the 1930 Hays Office Film Code.[8] But while *Pinky* is widely understood to be the first film to challenge the race bar, the legal cause of its censoring was prejudice, even as the plot is centered on miscegenation. The transfer between the themes of prejudice and miscegenation is suggestive: what seems to provoke a riotous white rage is not the prejudicial act by the white person, or even the salacious intentions of the Black man (one of the clear and present dangers perceived by white viewers of *Birth of a Nation*), but the intimation that white men might, by force or for love, be engaging in sexual acts across racial lines. But the white man who has transgressed racial hierarchy is not the object of the rage of white supremacist society. No, this hatred is directed—violently and repressively—toward Black people, especially Black women. In the white fictions of this period, the transgressive white man is represented as held captive by his "confused" desires and fearless refusal of prejudice as he stands by his passing woman (usually by advocating her deracialization, a possibility afforded by her relative lack of semiotic marks of Blackness and by her "manners," implicitly an inheritance of her whiteness). In the myriad dime novels and magazine versions of the passing woman's story, directed to a white female audience, the Black woman is held morally responsible for making the break away from the dreadful, problematic love.[9]

My intent here is to add depth to our understanding of the relationship between popular cultural offerings and our deeply felt senses of identity, but I also have an axe to grind with an academic debate—concerning "performativity"—that has had a major and, in my view, problematic impact on gender studies, lesbian and gay studies, and, to a much lesser extent, critical race theory. Inspired by two readings of Jacques Derrida's scant five-page deconstruction of J. L. Austin's (1975/1962) notion of the performative speech act (Sedgwick and Parker 1995; Butler 1990), a minor coterie of scholars in the 1990s threw themselves into analyses of identity, especially "queer" identities, as forms of reiteration. This analytic move was meant to contest the political and theoretical problems, noted by activists and scholars for various reasons, of assuming that identity is fixed and possibly socially, culturally, or biologically determined. Apparently innocent of the rich work on acting in performance studies (once a branch of theater studies) and on "practice of self in everyday life" (within both Goffman-influenced sociology [1963] and post-structural theories following de Certeau [1984]), scholars swept away in the performativity craze conflated—or, at any rate, failed to think much about the utility of maintaining as different—a concept drawn from speech act theory with a practice based in a millennium of thinking about how one appears to others. Before long, what might have been an interesting distinction was totally obfuscated. Judith Butler, one of the architects of performativity's voracious appetite, complained that most people wound up conflating performativity with commonsense notions of performance, rather than allowing the reverse compaction to foreground the problems in commonsense notions of pretending, playacting, etc.

Without conducting what would no doubt be an interesting genealogy of this line of thought, I note here that these discussions of identity collapsed the presentation of self in everyday life with *acting constituted as such*. While the former was indeed undergoing a certain reflexive moment (i.e., the critique of essentialism; the debate about the diffuse claim, proposed by feminists, that "the personal is political"), acting, as a cross-cultural and transhistoric social discipline, had always demanded an account of itself. Thus, instead of interrogating the larger conditions that sometimes oppose acting and life and make acting a vehicle for discovering life's truths, 1990s discussions of performative identity treated the analogy between performance and identity as necessary.

But acting has its histories too: even a casual Friday night mission to the DVD rental store makes obvious the variety of styles in film acting over the past hundred years. These acting genres, in tension with one another, change in relation to a variety of factors—what we might think of as the conditions of possibility for film acting: for example, changes in censorship laws and the beliefs about media effects that underwrote them; changes in sound and image technologies; changes in perceptions of what an actor's labor discloses to audiences.

As an important popular medium, movies and the vast discussion of them suggest when and how practical theories of acting become a means to secure and challenge social consensus on the significance of marked bodies. Suppression, double coding, and showcasing of particular forms of ethnicity or sexual difference suggest that acting styles at different times variously reflect, evade, or popularize particular notions of the relation between an "inner" and "outer" self, between a person and his or her social location or history. In my view, these changes in acting are not just performed by actors and discussed by critics. They are taken up by viewers as interpretive frames and bodily senses. When we say that someone is a good or bad actor, we are making a judgment about the competence of their labor in the context of what we believe their labor is supposed *to do*. We still judge movies against a discourse of realness and intersubjective transfer of "universal emotion" that was established in the period I am describing as the natural and appropriate form for "serious" drama. Indeed, the emergent acting style I identify in the problem films is premised on claims about the relationship of bodily sentiment and intersubjectivity; that is, Method acting is understood to replicate "real feelings" that are then communicated to the audience who then "experiences" them as proper to the context proposed in the diegesis of the film. This labels the "feelings" and, at least when employed in the social commentary films discussed here, prescribes a course of action that is seen as the proper outcome of "understanding the problem." As the audience is trained to align the acting style with their sentiments, they must take up the narrow framing of the "problem," in the case of the "Negro films," establishing a strongly held feeling about racism that only barely replaces an earlier feeling about race. As we will see in a moment, Method acting was initially experienced as jarring and was not well received by filmgoers, but it soon became the normalized style for dramatic film. Similarly, the antiacting style of Arnold Schwarzenegger was initially seen simply as bad acting, but the flat style and wry self-consciousness were eventually normalized as a post–cold war style of patriotic masculinity that replaced the somber cowboy and war movie standard of John Wayne. Indeed, Bill Clinton appeared (at least before the Lewinsky scandal) to have absorbed some of Schwarzenegger's "Gee wiz! I'm in a movie!" style with his perpetually beguiled delight at finding himself president,[10] a style that charmed many Americans who had grown cynical toward the overblown staginess of Ronald Reagan and the blatant disdain for ordinary Americans demonstrated by George Bush Sr., who "acted" like he didn't want to address us at all.

But it is dangerous to shift too seamlessly from movies to life.

As it turns out, all the world is not a stage, and, whether couch potatoes or Oscar winners, we are only actors on it sometimes. If performativity had a use (and I will refrain from using the term here for the sake of distinguishing my position), it was to mark the double constitution of self and place, to demand that we consider not only how we come across (for example, by claiming an identity over and over) but also how the conditions under which such presentations of self make sense also change and sometimes change under the force of "an" identity. Identity, perhaps we can all agree, is not a thing or even a necessity, but an accomplishment, and such a feat is always subject to constraints, even when a particular iteration exceeds previous expectations.

My curiosity, then, is not directed at the ways people copy identities, or the ways popular media present them, but rather toward the ways we come to understand "identity" and "interiority" as possibilities, and possibilities that have social and political implications. Without overstating the case regarding the new kind of identity enacted for audiences in the problem films, I want nonetheless to insist on these films as especially powerful "classrooms" for teaching (especially white Americans) how to apprehend Black personhood "inside" the Black body, and how to understand the possibilities that intersubjective movement between "identities" might hold for mitigating the hazards of plurality in a male- and white- and Christian-dominated society. Although I will devote most of this book to the discourse on acting that emerged regarding race (which included "Jewish" presentation as a race), I want to consider whether this discourse, routed in part through the interaction of the civil rights and gay liberation movements, also provided the condition of possibility for the ensuing discourse, not of gay and lesbian acting, but of acting lesbian or gay.

Race and Sexuality: Some Analytic Caveats

One of the fatal outcomes of this ill-considered turn in queer theory has been the temptation to analogize the mixed-race person— "the mulatto"—and the pre-identitarian queer. In particular, this amounts to viewing literary and cinematic representations of the former as doubling for the latter. The over-reading of queerness onto or into the mixed-race body has a partial basis in film censorship practices—both miscegenation and sexual perversion were proscribed. However, such readings fail to record that censorship practices understood these as different orders of sexual deviation, and I argue that they appear in film as different orders of sign. One cause of this analytic conflation of racial and queer undecidability is the overemphasis on racial hybridity and queerness as "secrets," as a narrative problem, rather than as a historically specific representational problem, as a specific form of unstable sign.[11]

Research on early-nineteenth-century sexology and phrenology suggests that the idea of locating a common cause for human difference is at least coextensive with film. However, seeing queer sensibility in the mixed-race body requires an associative logic that emerged only after lesbian and gay activists used the civil rights discourse upon which it was contingent to partially secure the civil and legal analogy between themselves and African Americans. Far from reflecting an existing double coding, the changes in film acting that troubled reviewers of the problem films helped lay the groundwork for that association. In essence, the very idea of identity as an interiority that cannot be fully hidden but can be partially intersubjectively sensed emerged in its particularly American form in the post–World War II period and, most popularly, in mass-market novels and movies.

This is not to say that no concept of identity appears before World War II; as Foucault has suggested, identity has a long genealogy, and there are particular shifts in the nineteenth century that lead to the idea, and to the felt reality, of an "inner self." Exactly what this self is and how it relates to other selves has been undergoing constitution since identity was born. Some writers have emphasized the importance of national identity in the modern period, viewing "personal identities" as derived from and less important than national identity. As we will see in the discussion of *Gentleman's Agreement,* it is inadequate to segment personal and social identities from national identities, not least because segmentation obscures the ways in which personal and social identities are marked by the same practices of governmentality that, in the obverse, explicitly demand particular styles of national identity. Thus, there is a peculiarly American version of personal identity that combines the American love of individualism with the recognition that older signs of persons—like race and ethnicity and class, but, in recent years, also gender and sexuality—are arbitrary and equivocal, said to be mostly secured by a feeling. What the problem films try to negotiate as they deconstruct and reconstruct racial signs, and as they argue for the similarity-in-difference of Americans, is the mode of *decoding* signs. Thus, a sign stimulates sight but also transforms looking into an intersubjective experience; the eyes are a window on the soul at the same time that they are a means of collecting semiotic data. This ambivalence toward the sign under conditions of plurality (in essence the problem Charles Peirce was working out at the turn of this recent century through his pragmatic semiology) took a very specific form in America: the melting pot, but not quite; the dual-party system, but not quite; the separation of church and state, but not quite.[12]

The difference between assuming a continuous historical analogy and demonstrating it becomes apparent in the theoretical missteps in the several articles published in the 1990s on Douglas Sirk's 1959 *Imitation of Life,* a jumping-off point for Judith Butler and subsequent writers' theorizing of the conjoint performativity of race and gender. These works fail to consider the specific technological, legal, and genre context of the film, elements that, I will suggest here, profoundly affect what "being Black on film" means and, in turn, what "understanding Blackness" means. One need only compare the Sirk version of *Imitation* to Stahl's 1934 version to realize that something had changed in Americans' concerns over the problem of race relations, and that acting—that is, the naturalization of a form of acting as "real"—was key to that change.

I would be the last person to suggest that popular culture artifacts cannot be treated as lush moments for much larger theorizing of race, gender, and sexuality. However, some artifacts are so deeply marked by the specificity of their conditions of production and reception that leaping too far from them obscures what is most important about them. The extraordinarily rare films about racial passing are such artifacts. White audiences seem to think *Imitation of Life* is about what it is like to pass. Actually, both versions, but especially the Sirk version, are about reactions *to* the passing person. *Pinky,* while also displaying reactions to muted racial coding, is remarkable in trying, however badly, to convey a sense of "what it's like" to pass and, via the character of Dicey, played by Ethel Waters, "what it's like" "to be" an African American woman whose experience and identity are continuous with the era of slavery, "what it's like" "to be" a postcolonial subject affectively tied to the persons and modalities of a now-past regime. As compared to the slick Sirk version of *Imitation, Pinky* occupies a much different place in the history of film and film censorship, in changing film technologies, and, most importantly, in the emergence of new forms of acting.

Readers with some time on their hands might settle in for a triple feature: Stahl's 1934 version of *Imitation,* Kazan's 1949 *Pinky,* and Sirk's 1959 version of *Imitation,* each produced at a crucial juncture in the history of acting. Stahl's *Imitation* was completed shortly after synchronized sound films came to dominate the industry, forcing actors to deliver dialogue while moving on the set. *Pinky* has a disorganized acting style, combining the pinnacle version of the classic style with the emergent Method acting. Crucially here, the Method style is used—brilliantly by Ethel Waters and the supporting cast of Black actors (for a listing of cast members, see the appendix), pathetically by Jeanne Crain—by actors whose authenticity as "Black" was partly produced through the citation of realness implicit in the style. Method was well established on stage before it was taken up in film and thus already connoted a hard look at real feelings. Even if audiences of mainstream movies had not seen Method on the stage, fan magazines—a central intertext connecting forms of culture—and movie reviews discussed Method-style researching of parts. At a crucial point in American history, this politicized the psychology of the Method, reinforcing the idea that basic human experiences—including "being oppressed"—could be universally sensed. The political nature of *Pinky*'s mishmash of styles was secured by the censoring of the film and, later, by the Supreme Court ruling regarding *Pinky* that was widely understood (somewhat incorrectly) to end nearly forty years of legal film censorship based on fears of race mixing. While it may have been the cinematic standout of the trio, Sirk's 1959 *Imitation* incorporated the acting innovations of the problem films, but only after they had been generalized as "serious drama" and depoliticized.[13]

But even the history of race-related censorship is more complicated than at first it seems, since race and sex are complexly intertwined in the evolving statutes and codes. By 1930, the Hays Code[14] completely proscribed both miscegenation and perversion as sexual signs, but these were not analogous because the problem with each was not of the same symbolic register. Either of two images, a couple comprised of a Black and a white person, or either of these with a mixed-race person could, respectively, iconically or indexically signify miscegenation, but only the iconic sign of the biracial couple was censored. In fact, the "mulatto" had a long film career as the figure of tragedy; but her[15] problem was her lack of place in a racially segregated society, not the rape of her probably Black mother, or the possibility that she, as Black by default, might suffer a similar fate in similar circumstances. The "tragic mulatto" was iconic, anxiously and insistently not indexical: her film presence consistently referred to her diegetic predicament, not the history that made sense of her as a historic referent.

By contrast, with no culturally secured referent, only indexical perversion was censored. According to Vito Russo (1981), the bulk of perversion-related cuts made to pre–World War II films had to do with improper gestures and poses, or situations and places (bars, beds, and embraces). Once sound combined dialogue and gesture, familiarity with presumed "gay terms" was added to the list. As with the mulatto, not all queerness was banned; homosexual tendencies were among the elements that might connote evil characters. In the dozen or so early films Russo identifies as having "gay" characters, homosexuality served as the most extreme means of ensuring fulfillment of a pivotal Hays Code mandate that "sympathy of the audience should never be thrown to the side of crime, wrongdoing, evil or sin."[16]

Although they were mutually implicated in early censorship provisions, Black personality and lesbian and gay characters later saw acceptance decades apart and through different genres. Authentic racial subjects were popularized through the work of Black Method actors and their successors; the very presence of James Edwards, Sidney Poitier, Hattie McDaniel, or Ethel Waters signaled that the film was "about race."[17] This popular discourse, which related an essential identity to a historical condition of oppression, was established well before the gay liberation—or even homophile—movements linked the adoption of identity with the quest for public visibility.

Although several films of the problem era grapple with homosexuality, authentic portrayal of gay characters had to wait until the 1980s, when popular discourse had produced a "real" referent from whom the straight actor could distance himself. In opposition to the conflation of Black bodies and Black acting, gay characters were available only after gay/lesbian identity was stabilized and actors could make the claim that they were *not* queer, and thus were not, like Poitier or Waters, "playing themselves." Popular accounts of the actors who have played gay roles emphasize their Method-like researching of the part as the source of their "authentic" portrayal. Tom Hanks's triumph in *Philadelphia* (1993) came in part because he could guarantee his distance from the character he portrayed; he *acted*. Although the style of acting for Black and gay characterizations has a similar look and feel, they are at opposite poles of a labor continuum. Black actors are conflated with their role, while straight actors play gay characters better than gay ac-

Figure 2. *Bookends in the history of Method acting: Sidney Poitier in* In the Heat of the Night *(1967) and Tom Hanks in* Philadelphia *(1993).*

tors. Although all forms of difference are interrelated—at least to the extent that they are other to a common hegemonic identity—this obvious variation in the modality of acting the differences raises serious questions about current approaches that cross-read race and sexuality.

Acting the Citizen

During the mid-1940s through mid-1950s Americans voiced new concern about the race problem or the color bar. In contrast to the virulent post–World War II anticommunism—a concern focused on the foreign and international—racism was constructed as a domestic problem. The categorization of racism within the new structure of governmentality corresponds to the increasing division between the domestic and national/international spheres (often called the feminization of government) that issued from the quasi-socialization of certain government welfare functions that occurred during the New Deal years. Although this understanding of the nature and solution to racism seemingly set racism and communism as problems existing in difference spheres, the two were nevertheless rhetorically and politically conjoined. Radicals argued that communism or socialism offered a solution to racism, while liberals co-opted this idea to frame a progressive anticommunism, which suggested that any failure to deal with domestic racism would leave America open to infiltration by communists. Although American socialists and communists had long grappled with the promise of new political ideas for ameliorating America's long legacy of racism (mainly its anti-Semitic and anti-Black, not so much its anti-Asian and anti-aboriginal ideologies), the post–World War II era saw a new and particular response in "the Southland," a term one member of the House Committee on Un-American Activities used persistently to refer to the states that once comprised the Confederacy.[18] A dual construction of the American South as a place and as the residual space of segregationist and states' rights political sentiments was very much at the heart of the reconstruction of communism in the 1950s.[19] Thus, the 1958 HUAC trials held in Atlanta provide special insight into post–World War II antiracist/anticommunist analysis that shaped the civil rights movement and the radical left, student, and antiwar movements of the 1960s.[20]

In the following two chapters, I will trace the contours of the affective relationship to nation that I argue emerged in the post–World War II era—a relationship that forms the apparently natural subjectivity on which citizenship is built. To do so, I will examine three areas where I believe this relationship took shape: in the rhetoric of the 1948–52 revision of immigration and naturalization statutes and the book-to-film project of *Gentleman's Agreement* (1947); in the proceedings, mandate, and reactions to the House Committee on Un-American Activities (1958); and in the effective termination of the film code in 1952. Using these locations, I show how the notion of citizenship was reconstructed from the warrior-buddy citizen-soldier into an empathetic masculinity that could "walk in the other guy's shoes" without falling prey to communist-like loss of individual identity. Meanwhile, the HUAC hearings helped establish the restricted categories within which subsequent social movements, up to the gay liberation movement, would be permitted to thrive.

From its first mass distribution, film was understood to have a complex of effects on audiences, but I will discuss the importance of sexual desire and criminal impulse as the two most feared reactions. Intra-industry codes struggled from the beginning to define what was appropriate in film, with the hopes of forestalling the state censorship seen in other countries. *Pinky* would become one of the films that pressed the question of race-based prohibitions, but the role of interracial sexual desire and other forms of "perversion" were complexly linked in the court findings. Once I establish a sense of the complex of discursive and regulatory changes that comprise this critical transitional period from hot to cold war, I will explore the role of acting in the constitution of a new way to feel and be a white American.

2

IN THE HEARTS OF MEN

It might not be The American Century after all,
or The Russian Century, or The Atomic Century.
Perhaps it would be the century that broadened and
implemented the idea of freedom, all the freedoms.
Of all men.

— Laura Z. Hobson, *Gentleman's Agreement*

Published in the midst of cold war paranoia about world communism, the wildly popular *Gentleman's Agreement* (1946; film 1947) inaugurated the paradoxical companion trend of contending with America's domestic problems through popular entertainment. Set against an agon figured on one hand as a contest between Russia and America and, on the other, as The Horror from which we could no longer retreat (the fantasized atomic holocaust, not the actual racist-genocidal ones), these apparently progressive entertainments directed their moral appeal not to nation but to humanity. And yet, the idea of humanity evoked by such films and novels was itself already shot through with the American dread of communism. Indeed, the texts struggle with how to manage domestic conflict without rendering the fabric of nation-ness susceptible to alien influences and threats. As the merits of a global defense of democracy faded for the many people who were locked out of the American Dream, one means of securing new allegiance to nation was the heavy broadcasting of the House Committee on Un-American Activities (HUAC) hearings.

As we know, gay people were increasingly targeted as the hearings progressed. In addition to shattering individual lives, the hearings had negative consequences for subsequent gay politics in at least three ways: they caused a split in the early homophile movement; they sharpened the tooth of immigration and government employment policies based on the equation of closeted homosexuals (at risk of giving away state secrets) and hidden communists (actively betraying America); and, at least until the 1960s, they became the historical backdrop that structured all of the new social movements' relations to Marxist theory and practice. A momentous, dark moment indeed.

Foucault admonished us not to think of power as purely negative, unitary, and crushing down from above, but also as productive, multiple, lateral. Looking back across the last four decades, it is clear that while homosexuals were swept up in the HUAC feeding frenzy, they were also added to the category of those "problems" toward which Americans might turn a gentler eye. Indeed, HUAC plays a complicated role in gay history. Part of the bargain of civil rights, once they were secured by new laws and practices in the 1960s, was the demand for a legible history of oppression. Once HUAC was widely accepted as one of America's ugliest hours, lesbians and gay men could point to the hearings as vivid evidence of homosexuals' status as a "suspect class."[1] However, a critical issue of queer historicity emerges in this particular instance of historicization of lesbian and gay oppression. Since gay people did not form a coherent civil class until the late 1980s (and this is still highly contentious, as Janet Halley [1993] has shown), who or what was under attack by HUAC?

I contend that unlike the red-baiter's object of disdain, the communist—understood as alien to the nation—the 1940s queer was still *of* the nation. In the transformation of the citizen under way in the post–World War II era, homosexuals were not so much another kind of invader—virtual aliens owing to their relationship to another nation—as they were the limit case of a new kind of citizenship that required empathy, but not to the extent of replacing the nation as love object.[2]

That queerness would have been incorporated into the national project of redefining the citizen is counterintuitive considering that anticommunist and antihomosexual sensibilities were palpable elements of post–World War II American identity, albeit to different degrees. Indisputably, the rhetoric of the HUAC trials and, as I have myself shown (Patton 1995a), of more recent right-wing homophobes, employs metaphors of penetration and invasion to describe the danger of both communism and queerness. But the place of queerness in the rhetoric of the post–World War II years is still different, and this has had important consequences for subsequent gay politics. It is easy to see the direct effect of the heavy-handed HUAC trials on the individual lives of those who stood in its bizarre path. More difficult to register is the subtle reconfiguration of the very idea of citizenship upon which the civil rights efforts of the second half of the twentieth century would rest. The fixity of the class "communist" should not mislead us into presuming that the reasons for objecting to homosexuals—not yet officially discursively constructed as a class—ran in parallel. Both communist association and homosexuality were reasons for exclusion of aliens under immigration law.[3] But queerness was not taken as a serious demonstration of political allegiance to some other world order, a difference that added potency to an important distinction between kinds of problems: "soft" social ones (exemplified by homos) and "hard" political ones (exemplified by commies). In addition, the geography imagined as the location of homosexual invasion and the physics of the dimension of reality in which the nation's sexual perimeter was imagined to exist were completely different than those that were under assault by communists.

I have suggested elsewhere (Patton 1993; 1995a) that the very idea of identity as we think if it now is inextricably bound to the rise of civil rights law, with its need to set the parameters of a suspect class by isolating the trait that forms the basis for systematic discrimination of a class. I extend that argument now to contend that this trait identification process involved an affective restructuring of white Americans based on conjoined worries about communism with the need to shift from a war-based connection to nation to a social cohesion-based connection; that is, from an affect directed through nation to one directed through society. I do not suppose that the support for the civil rights movement, much less the later establishment of homosexual's class status,[4] happened solely through the efforts of countless civil rights activists. Nor do I imagine that the history of oppression, invoked as the aura of lesbian and gay classness, arrived in the mind of America unmediated. A concept of minority "experience" similar to that described by activists as "consciousness" was first popularized in novels and films of the post–World War II era. Activists viewed these new consciousnesses among the myriad oppressed as harbingers of revolutionary change. But in popular culture, "experience," a new zone for mutual understanding, and "identification" via mediated access to the experience of others, enthusiastically promised to quell domestic troubles.

America's long-standing, perhaps nationally constitutive mixed feelings about social issues were intrinsically biased toward, or rather, positioned in relation to, "who one was" and what cross-identifications one was willing to take on. As traumatic as race relations were (and there were not only race riots in many cities, but also lynchings), without outside agitators White America did not see its domestic race relations as a threat to America as a nation; social issues were *problems,* not politics. In the postwar period, America developed a new faith that lowering the boundaries of the ego in order to merge with another—the imaginary practice of identification rather than the socio-sexual practice of *mixing*—would forever change Americans' empathy toward one another. The techniques of such a new citizenship were demonstrated through Method acting (see chapter 4)—already popular on the stage and entering cinema through the problem films—and in a new style of journalism that shed strict objectivity in favor of placing the reader, or even the person of the reporter (just recall *Black Like Me* [Griffin 1962]), in the scene. I want to explore the production of the empathetic citizen and the reconstruction of his (principally[5]) affective relation to nation and comrade through a consideration of a legal distinction between kinds of aliens, the surprising use of a female entertainment as a political vehicle, and the specific construction of the anti-anti-Semite.

To Die For

In the epidemiology of the Red Scare, gay communists were assigned to the active, masculinized category, "communist," both
confounding and reifying the equation of the two. There were, of
course, many antigay communists and not a few anticommunist
gays, but for the HUAC senators, vilification of one did not exonerate
those accused of the other; the true American was neither. HUAC
struggled to reorganize love of country and love of fellow man. The
wrong degree of either was problematic, but for different reasons.
In fact, the communist who wanted a world order and the homosexual who preferred love of fellow citizens to love of nation were
opposites that constituted a third term: the anticommunist citizen
with appropriate empathy toward others. According to Public Law
414 (PL 414), also known as the Immigration and Nationality Act
of 1952,[6] the problem with communism—a problem also latent in
Zionism, popularly misunderstood as a religion that could supplant the nation—was its terrifying global ambitions:

> Sec. 101 (a) (40) The term "world communism" means a revo-
> lutionary movement, the purpose of which is to establish even-
> tually a Communist totalitarian dictatorship in any or all of the
> countries of the world through the medium of an internation-
> ally coordinated political movement. (PL 414, 171)

This long, elaborate statute on immigration, debated during
the early years of HUAC (concurrently with the court's hearing
of both *Brown v. Board of Education* [347 U.S. 483, 1954, hereafter
Brown v. Board of Education] and the several film censorship cases
that are said to have ended film censorship) and finally passed in
1952, concretizes the communist hunters' sensibility into contemporary American law[7] and hints at the difference between queerness and communism in the different responses it offers to aliens
of these two kinds.

Though mute on the issue of how American-born communists would be treated (with the spectacular exception of the exe-
cuted Rosenbergs they were harassed, but not literally exiled[8]),
Public Law 414 is quite clear that to declare oneself communist

is to make oneself inadmissible to the United States. The declaration of homosexuality could also render one inadmissible, but the violation of American law was different. Indeed, the sections pertaining to allegiance toward the idea of a world political order or to communism are copious and repeated at every juncture to ensure no escape hatches, while the sections attending to immoralities are relatively brief and nonrepetitive, as if they are self-evident and easy to apply. Public Law 414 accords different status to political membership or advocacy than it does to immorality. In this understanding, apparently, immoralities are apolitical. While they inhere in the individual—perhaps unbeknownst to him—and will eventually surface, they are a problem of social order, not of political sovereignty. By contrast, an individual's politics, explicitly known to the holder of such beliefs, are structured on the logic of deniability; the ability to strategically deny one's beliefs implies that they are already conscious to the self. Immoralities are private truths that will eventually speak, even if only through mannerisms and desires that make public a love that knows not its name. But political beliefs, because they are lodged in the conscious, are resistant to what Foucault (1990/1978) called the incitement to discourse.[9] Thus, the law must enumerate the objective signs of membership that no denial could override. While some have to do with actually speaking a doctrine, most are at some remove, consolidating and accelerating this interest in tracking financial affairs:[10]

> The giving, loaning, or promising of support or of money or any other thing of value to be used for advocating any doctrine shall constitute the advocating of such doctrine; . . .

> . . . giving, loaning, or promising of support or money or any other thing of value for any purpose to any organization shall be presumed to constitute affiliation therewith; . . .

> Advocating the economic, international, and governmental doctrines of world communism means advocating the establishment of a totalitarian Communist dictatorship in any or all of the countries of the world. . . . (Sec. 101, 40e, 1, 2, 3; 172)

This advocacy or affiliation is a reason for nonadmission to America because it exposes a person's citizenlike relation to a supranational world order intrinsically challenging to U.S. national integrity. Critically, the zeal for exposing financial networks notwithstanding, the ability to distinguish between moral and immoral, patriots and traitors who disguised their beliefs, rested on a feeling— left unexplained in the law but elaborated in popular stories like *Gentleman's Agreement.*

By contrast, homosexuality is implied within a subsequent section (101, f, 1–8; 172) that enumerates the specific areas to be examined in determining whether a person is of "good moral character," a task to be accomplished only after a petitioner's national allegiance had been established.[11] Here, the worry is that such persons might burden the welfare state, swell the ranks of criminals, or, in the case of prostitution and the seeking of perverse sexual acts, subtly tear at the fabric of American domestic life. But precisely because they are not political, suspect sexual bodies presented a special problem: as vivid as was the Fear of a Commie Planet, communists' allegiance was still to a world political order, a kind of mega-nation that strengthened the idea of nations, united or not. By contrast, homosexuals defied the very primacy of nation as the ultimate love object.

There are many ways of aligning love of country and love of man. Long before they imagined themselves a queer "nation," long before proto-identitarian homosexuals like Edward Carpenter conceptualized specifically queer politics, Western political philosophers like Plato had imagined various homosocial/erotic bonds as the basis of patriotism. However, during the immediate post– World War II era, American politicians of the right asserted that the degraded desire of one man to consume another's body had the power to undermine that most noble desire: to surrender one's body and die for one's nation. They might have suggested, as some far-right politicians do today, that self-annihilation was the homosexual's patriotic duty. But America was unwilling to be officially and completely rid of its homosexual citizens; exclusion from direct contact with the important business of the state was enough. The emerging civil rights efforts (collectively emitting a shudder at the idea of including sexuality as a category) and immigration law (which was not interested in separating homosexuality as a "preference" or "orientation" from other immoral sex acts) were ambivalent about the etiology and effects of two directions of political love: comrade-love and nation-love. Despite the quick slide that made American communists virtual Russians and American Jews virtual Zionists, America declined to construe American homosexuals as virtual aliens, as patriots responding to a different national drum.

I want to consider for a moment Benedict Anderson's idea of political love in order to make the point that the historical narratives that emphasize the apparent liberalization of social attitudes in post–World War II America obscure the complex reorganization of the structure of the citizen's affectivity, a change that both enabled the "tolerance" of difference observable in the 1960s–90s and also fastened the fundamental class and religious politics to a no-less-problematic "feeling" of moral righteousness that could find its logic played out in the dismantling of Black voting, the Defense of Marriage Act, and the back-to-back Iraq wars. Anderson's *Imagined Communities* (1991/1983) has been extended and reworked to analyze different forms of media/tion that have produced the variety of forms of nation we know today. But it is the affective relation to the nation, more even than its heterogeneity, that seems upon closer reading to be Anderson's central concern. He ponders "why, today, they command such profound emotional legitimacy" (4), and he returns to this problematic after detailing—and so nearly causing us to lose sight of affectivity— the multiple and historically contingent forms that imagining a nation takes.[12]

> The great wars of this century are extraordinary not so much in the unprecedented scale on which they permitted people to kill, as in the colossal numbers persuaded to lay down their lives . . .

> Dying for one's country, which usually one does not choose, assumes a moral grandeur which dying for the Labour Party, the American Medical Association, or perhaps even Amnesty International can not rival, for these are all bodies one can join or leave at easy will. Dying for the revolution also draws its grandeur from the degree to which it is felt to be something

fundamentally pure. (If people imagined the proletariat *merely* as a group in hot pursuit of refrigerators, holidays, or power, how far would they, including members of the proletariat, be willing to die for it?) (144)

Because the form of nation is multiple, a nationality is not reducible to the simultaneity of a mark and inhabitation of a single place. Even the historico-ethnic similarity of a people who've happened to alight in the same place fails to reliably mark nationality. Rather, Anderson seems to be saying, it is this willingness to die for an abstraction, fixed in space and/or time as "nation," that forms the basis of modern nation-feeling. Recognizing this complex love that binds together historically divergent formations of nation in peace and war clarifies why the homosexual, under the regime of rights discourse that emerged in post–World War II America, could neither be assimilated to nor ejected from the nation, except by allowing religion to momentarily trump the State. The homosexual appears to share many of the traits of the citizen, often including overt patriotism. He does not direct his allegiance to another nation; he is still, legally, American. The geo-phagic logic of nation cannot imagine a body without a nation and, unlike its Spartan precursor, the nation refuses to accept that love of men over country might mean that the citizen is willing to die in war not *for* nation but *as* lover. The problem with the homosexual's love is dual: either he is acting in the interest of something that he can "join or leave at easy will" (the contemporary "choice" rhetoric); or he is engaged in an allegiance that is not fundamentally pure, not because it violates some biblical passage, but because its unnaturalness, though not chosen, is nonetheless not a "natural" tie. To understand homosexuality's problematic relation to nation we can recall Anderson's discussion of political love, which

> . . . can be deciphered from the ways in which languages describe its object: either in the vocabulary of kinship (motherland, *Vaterland*, *patria*) or that of home (*heimat* or *tanah air* [earth and water, the phrase for the Indonesian's native archipelago]). Both idioms denote something to which one is naturally tied. As we have seen earlier, in everything "natural" there is always something unchosen. In this way, nation-ness is

assimilated to skin-color, gender, parentage and birth-era—all those things one can not help. And in these "natural ties" one senses what one might call "the beauty of *gemeinschaft.*" To put it another way, precisely because such ties are not chosen, they have about them a halo of disinterestedness. (143)

Following Foucault, most cultural (studies) theorists argue that in the modern period, the understanding of homosexual acts shifts from a legal discourse concerned with criminal behavior to a moral discourse concerned with human essence, with homosexual-*ity*. This person-state is at once essential and unnatural, a pitiable condition that cannot be helped and that renders the modern homosexual—especially the post–World War II American homosexual—a fractured citizen; his desire to love man over country is seen as a passive rejection of the political love that underwrites modern nationality. Because he cannot straighten out his love (at best, it vacillates between two objects), he is an unreliable citizen. Worse yet, this passive but corrosive homosexual desire is the abjection of an emergent masculinity that dares not speak its name but instead names what it refuses.[13] Although compared to the communist in later historical analyses, the homosexual of this period emerges not as a communistlike invader pursuing a new world order but as a figure possessing an obsessive, neurotic masculinity that has failed to integrate its various subnational identifications into a national identity. Post–World War II masculinity had to be unified if it was to embrace the mantle of world leader, protector of a democracy that demanded pluralizing—a tough job for the latter-day version of Teddy Roosevelt's Rough Riders. Critical to this precarious pluralism was the ability of the universal to "understand" the particular as also partaking in humanity; that is, to mobilize the claim that "we're all God's children," the new national identity had to maintain certain marks (white, male, Christian, eventually heterosexual) as proper to The Universal in order for that universal to better understand its Other than the particular could understand itself. The question of the subaltern's ability to understand the colonizer (a central area of theorization in postcolonial studies) did not even enter into the equation, since to admit that the particular could already grasp the Universal was incompatible with the positionality under constitution for the white, heterosexual, Christian male. But recognizing the inaccessible knowledge already existing in the Other's epistemological space is, I will argue in chapter 5, the critical "sense" that would underwrite a real pluralism, as opposed to the always- and ever-condescending pluralism of those who recirculate their power through the pretext that the Universal is more capable of understanding than the particular.[14] Learning to "walk in the other guy's shoes," the homoerotic slip that is the popular phrasing of a New Testament parable, ushered in a treacherous new kind of masculinity as the basis for a new American identity: the covert subject position from which the Universal could, through a more or less one-way system of intersubjective communication, "read" the particular. What was partly at stake in the vilification of homosexuals was the interiority of the citizen; indeed, who knew what—evil or good—lurked in the hearts of men? Equally important: who was going to find out? The lingering fear that it takes one to know one is partly dampened by the new conviction, rampant in postwar university English departments and popular entertainment, that art, as a medium for transferring experience, could be put to work solving America's melting pot problem. The most domestic genre—melodrama—seemed the likely place to enact this "domestic problem"—the transfer of national attention from world war to social issues.

Popularizing "the Problem": Politics as Melodrama

In the 1940s, the problem novel and film emerged (not unlike slave narratives in an earlier era) as enormously popular entertainments. Although the films, and to a less obvious extent, the novels to which they relate, span a range of formally defined genres—action films (*Home of the Brave* 1949), noir (*Crossfire* 1947), and melodrama *(Gentleman's Agreement* 1947 and *Pinky* 1949)—commentators of the day and subsequent historians have written about them as a quasi-genre whose distinguishing commonality is thematic rather than formal. Historians of these works generally cite a supposed postwar liberalization of social attitudes as the impetus for the sudden popularity of books and films about long-standing American problems. Film historians especially describe the apparently incremental exploration of the problems America was imagined as newly willing to examine, echoing the sense of the relative difficulty of coming to grips with each that is explicit in the works themselves: anti-Semitism, racism, and the final frontiers of homosexuality, drug addiction, and, eventually, gender relations (Winnington 1976). Or, as a character in *Gentleman's Agreement* puts it: "What the hell chance have we of getting decent with 13 million Negroes if we can't lick the much easier business of anti Semitism?" (1946). However formally different the films within a genre are, commentators' and historians' sense that audiences were newly open to controversial topics binds the works into a mutually referential block, a genre defined by its ambition to enlighten post–World War II Americans and to modernize their attitudes toward "social" issues. But the emphasis on theme leads most commentators to overlook interrelated aspects of the books and films and their reception—in particular, their self-conscious attention to the psychological structuring of prejudice and bigotry and their presumption that forms of oppression are, if harder and easier to cope with, substantively interchangeable. There is an uncomfortable and unspoken premise that an individual's pathological prejudice looms larger than the systems and structures that maintain white middle-class-ness against variegated difference.

Home of the Brave (1949) was an early vehicle for James Edwards, a brilliant actor and later president of the Screen Actors Guild. Edwards plays a Black soldier undergoing psychoanalysis after he has become psychosomatically paraplegic following his unsuccessful attempt to save the racist Southerner whom he has befriended. The film is based on a book about a Jewish soldier dealing with anti-Semitism. The link between racism and anti-Semitism remains, or rather, is displaced: the Army psychiatrist who cures the soldier is heavily coded as Jewish.[15] Although flashback scenes make the work as a whole look like an action film, *Home of the Brave* is mostly about transference and counter-transference between victims and victimizers. Similarly, the very B-rated film noir *Crossfire* (1947) was based on a book (*The Brick*

Foxhole [1945]) about a homophobic murder. In the film, an offending Jew is killed early on, leaving a range of still homosexually-panicky B-movie hunks to display their anti-Semitism as they attempt to cover up their crime. While *Gentleman's Agreement* makes no similar substitution, the plot, in which Gregory Peck plays a Gentile reporter passing as a Jew in order to expose anti-Semitism, lifts a page from the popular stories of Black women passing as white, of which *Pinky*, released two years later, is the central cinematic example.[16]

Both the book and film version of *Gentleman's Agreement* rely on a new vision of the journalist as the producer of material that could be used to disentangle the crossed disidentification that is prejudice. The journalist is near and far—up close and personal with the prejudice he seeks to expose, but also distant and objective because he possesses, and models to the audience, the new universalist subjectivity under development in the post–World War II period. Thus, his close encounters call the citizen to a higher order of identification, not with a race or religion, but with a universal human experience of suffering and compassion. The practice of reverse passing is the most extreme means available for the sensitive socially dominant individual (or more likely his or her journalist surrogate, as in this fictional case and the later autobiography of reverse passing, *Black Like Me* [1962]) to achieve an "experience" that would transform his or her understanding of an Other. While literary theorists and college presidents debated the value of literature as a means to combat the anomie of modern life and the decay of a commonly held American sensibility, popular journalism was acculturating its readers to a "you are there" style of reporting that promoted the pseudo-interiority penned by reporters as a truth greater and simpler than that of the Great Works. Indeed, the reporter in *Gentleman's Agreement* (perhaps here speaking for author Laura Z. Hobson) describes his work this way:

> It was only a matter of disguising a name, a face, the background, but for the rest it was recording instead of contriving. Each thing as it had happened was put down; he was only the biographer of a Phil Green who was Jewish. The power of the inventing novelist or the devising playwright was a nothing

to this simple strength of the biographer; here was truth, not fantasy, here in these paragraphs unrolling were only fact and record. (Hobson 1946, 203)

By the end of the 1940s, the idea of "being there," recently secured for the war or international correspondent,[17] was applied more widely to reportage on domestic and extragovernmental issues and later resulted in a long-running children's educational book series about American history entitled "If You Were There" (Simon & Schuster Children's Publishing). The new style of journalism joined with melodrama to produce a new kind of entertainment that was controversial both in content and form. The reemergence of sentimental journalism paralleled the emergent style of war reporting; if the epic structure of the battle between good and evil made the war narrative coherent, then the melodrama rested on, and extended the audience for, an emotional repertoire for apprehending and being anxious about America's domestic troubles.

"Serious" films would soon be able to drop the journalist intermediary as the audience's vehicle for cross-identifications. Method acting, which rests on a similar commitment to the pseudo-autobiographic,[18] would eventually signal to the dominant viewer that cross-identification for the purpose of "better understanding" was not only permitted but encouraged. The flat-footedness, the "queerness" of these early cinematic attempts to forge a new structure of identification comes less from bad acting than from the redundancy of foregrounding the process of accessing one's "interiority," a stock in trade naturalized through Method. Method, the new style of journalism, and the legibility of melodrama's structure converged to form a new sensibility for interpreting social problems, but this collision jeopardized the gender divide of conventional entertainment forms.

Melodrama is widely understood—by consumers and academic critics alike—to be aimed at a female audience. Some reviewers in the 1940s revealed their perceptions of the gendering of political responsibility when they argued that it demeaned the seriousness of the problems to treat them through melodrama.[19] The disdain toward the political value of women's entertainment

Figure 3. *Gentile reporter Gregory Peck goes undercover as Jewish Phil Green in* Gentleman's Agreement *(1947). In his "walk in the other guy's shoes," Green is shocked to experience bigotry from the inside, including his discovery that a Jewish childhood friend, Dave Goldman (John Garfield), has been denied housing by racist landlords.*

continued in later commentators' criticism of melodrama's capacity to represent the truth of racism and anti-Semitism: David Cook (1981) believes that *Pinky*, as a "sentimental tale of a young Black woman who tries to pass for white, is even less credible [than *Gentleman's Agreement*]" (26).

That so many of the popular works about problems came in the form of melodrama is not an accident, but it may not be immediately obvious why this happened. The location of the represented troubles and the assignment of responsibility for their redress would be the subject of academic study and policy debate for at least three more decades, consolidated as affirmative action, civil rights, and welfare by the 1970s, and then undone. On one hand, the immediate post–World War II era saw a return to the cult of domesticity; women were rapidly transformed from industrial workers for the war machine into domestic managers of the consumer durables—fashioned, of course, in the factories in which these same women had beaten, smelted, and welded the very same materials into battleships. Women might have become the postmodern version of post-(American) colonial Mothers of the Republic—the central audience for politicizing "social" problems. However, as I will show below, women were actually excluded from the emerging idea of the citizen. The "war at home" had no place for women, whose job as keepers of consumerism was represented not as political action but as a distraction from political matters.[20] The government's role in the domestic life of the nation had already been "feminized" during the Great Depression; safety net social programs reached an unprecedented level and were classified as a function of central government. In the post–World War II era a more subtle refiguration was underway, concerned not so much with the government's role inside the borders of nation as with a reorganization of the citizen's self-policing of social conflict: how should we balance the citizen's vigilance against alien invaders with the need to dampen attention to the differences within the body politic that seemed to cause civil strife?

The production of the problem through melodrama is significant not simply because of audience demographics[21] but also because it suggests that learning about the new social problems would occur less through direct experience or political debate than through acquisition of the proper emotions and structures of identification. The proposed affectivity was both a blessing and a curse, a solution and a new problem. Intrinsic to the construction of social (as opposed to political) issues for the entertainment-consuming national public was a conviction that cross-identification would ultimately result in social progress. However, racial segregation was still the law, and "mixing" still held frightening connotations for whites. Expansion of mass media made it possible, even desirable, to promote an imaginary social equality—the domestic multicultural equivalent of the global village, but with the systems that make individual prejudice politically effective intact.[22] Indeed, what the problem worked to produce was a new definition of the citizen as one who could identify with the other members of the melting pot without actually taking responsibility for the various forms of privilege that skin color, sex, religion, and proximity to the norm afforded. Thus, *Gentleman's Agreement* casts an "actual" Gentile as a Gentile passing as a Jew, raising the question of whether Jews or "goys" could mistake a goy for a goy, or whether anyone would actually try such a ruse. Here, however, Kazan produces a *direct* line to goys: they can follow Peck's naïve outrage, knowing they don't actually have to experience anti-Semitism; they can distance themselves from many of the more subtle forms of anti-Semitism in which they engage by experiencing them vicariously as abjection, deploying the New Testament admonition to walk in another's shoes instead of the Old Testament law of revenge. For Jewish-identifying audience members, to the extent that they are considered, Peck could be a placeholder; they do not need to identify with him in order to reexperience anti-Semitism: "That happened to *me!*" Goy viewers are distanced from their own anti-Semitism as they learn to identify with Jewish experience. Jewish viewers, by co-occupying space with Peck rather than through him, need not question the central premise that goys will learn to be kinder and gentler through mediated understanding of the Other—an experience this film (and *Pinky*) represents as the product of beliefs. Effectively, what *Gentleman's Agreement* provides is a blueprint for transforming unwitting bigots into citizens with an aptitude for empathy who can know all about "others" without ever meeting "them."[23]

Into the Closet

Most of the widely circulated Hobson books are organized around the idea of journalism and the journalist as the site and personification of the truth about America. But this was a new kind of journalism, a journalism not of complete removal of bias but of passion and affectivity, the information equivalent of Method acting. After searching for an angle for his series on anti-Semitism, Phil Green, the protagonist in *Gentleman's Agreement*, realizes he'll "have to go at it from *inside*" (Hobson 1946, 72), be "Jewish for three months. . . . Or six weeks or however long, till I get the feel of it" (72). Despite his worries that his attempt to pass as a Jew is fraudulent Phil sometimes forgets he is only in character:

"'Funny thing,' he said, 'the way I felt so man-to-man with Miss Wales [a passing Jew] when she pitched me [an anti-Semitic remark]. Asking her right out how she felt, as if we both were really on the inside. I keep forgetting it's just an act'" (106).

As a new kind of journalist, Phil, who has previously gone undercover as a miner and a migrant worker, has the right combination of personal disinterestedness and a neurotic, queer capacity to "understand the other fellow." This affectivity is the postmodern relative of the modern conviction that Eve Kosofsky Sedgwick (1985) recognizes in the apt phrase that it takes one to know one. Here, the empathetic social chameleon politicizes instead of demonizes the man with the special sensitivity to temporarily lose himself to the other. In fact, such an individual might be able to capture an experience better than others who have lived it their whole lives. The non-Jew passing as a Jew is more objective; the actual, particular Jew is desensitized to and, in a sinister reintroduction of the stereotype under attack, hypersensitive to anti-Semitism. It is both his lack of defenses and his lack of group investment that makes the (Gentile) journalist the best person to report on the experience of this other: "identification" can reveal the essence of an experience that is mired in the individual pathologies (paranoia and overidentification) of those who have actually lived it.[24]

Like the 1990s television series *Quantum Leap* (1989–93), *Gentleman's Agreement* is loathe to admit that it is actually about the white man's burden of becoming nicer toward those whom he has exploited. Displacing the history of Christian white men's disastrous global escapades, Phil is a model of the type of person who alone has the capacity for the transformation that marks the new citizen, the one who will turn America from a sea of bigots into a nation of empaths. Granting present readers' inescapable association of the images employed here with the now-overdetermined relation between semen, HIV, and homosexuality, Phil's account of his transformation nevertheless reads like the aftermath of an unexpected, even unwanted, but exhilarating sexual encounter. Emotions are slightly unpleasant, an unformed goo. Experience enters the body through a portal other than the brain and becomes inseparably mixed with cells that are more properly one's own.

Gluey and inescapable, the extraordinary melancholy clung to him. . . . Phil tried to locate the source of this new infection of moodiness—the inn, his mother's stroke, the hostility of Miss Wales, the continued fruitlessness of Dave's search for a place to live, the postponement of the wedding—but not any one of them, nor the sum of them all, convinced him that he had isolated the cause of the sticky sadness in him.

He had accepted the fact that in a few weeks he'd undergone a swift and deep transfusion into his own blood of a million corpuscles of experience and emotion. (Hobson 1946, 182)

This identification just shy of identity loss, this emotional miscegenation, was a crucial moment in the desperate gambit to acquire the skills of a new citizenship; the new affectivity that enables the split between national-political and domestic-political, or as Phil's mother repeatedly admonishes him, "each home decides." Offering an alternate, but still complementary, solution to HUAC's hysteria, this new system of identification is the best plan against communism; it humanizes and individualizes the citizen in a way that "world orders" will not. Implicitly, it says that what makes an American is the capacity to produce and order emotions in service of freedom:

Jobs and economic security, sure—even the Fascists and Communists promise that. No, [publisher Minify] said it had got down to a matter of equal self-respect, pride, ego, whatever. Take Communism. It's got one good thing, anyway—equality among white and black, all minorities—only the price there is so big, too. If we did it, without the price of free speech, free opposition, free everything—then we'd really be fighting the Communists where it counts . . . beating antisemitism [sic] and antinegroism is a political must now, not just sweet decency. (184)

To some extent, the book depends on class stereotypes of masculinity, in which prejudice is situated "in a dark crackpot place with low-class morons" (192). The implicit masculinity of "obvious" anti-Semites helps make it easier to imagine the empathetic citizen not as feminized but as combating a dangerous form of masculinity. In the shift from decency to national security that partially sutures social issues to the task of beating the communists, liberal pluralism joins hands with the red-baiting that, if recognized as a dimension of racial or class conflict, it would have opposed. The paranoid political fantasy of unseen threats to America, which we tend to associate with the right, was front and center in the ethic adopted by post–World War II liberals:

> Millions [of people who don't think they are anti-Semitic] back up the lunatic vanguard in its war for this country—forming the rear echelons, the home front in the factories, manufacturing the silence and acquiescence. (192)

This careful re-inscription of the appropriate amount of masculinity[25] quietly sets itself against woman; her role in capitalist consumption and her emotions, which lead to confusion rather than transformation, exclude her from the sensitivities required of the new citizen. Though "subterranean," her emotions do not have the "goo" that sticks to man and transforms him:

> The subterranean paths that twined through human impulses and motives always eluded you if you tried to follow them. At least for her they did. There was no use to will herself to the task. She never had a road map. She always got lost. (88)

The patriotic male bond encourages identification across comparatively small social differences in order to stave off the dramatic difference that can be recognized in the company of women. This gulf separates empathy from emotion, reconstructs identification as a masculine activity that connects buddy-love not to desire or sexuality but to defense of country. Women who were enlisted into jobs during the war, like Phil's fiancée Kathy, are no longer part of a war effort à la the heroic image of Rosie the Rivetter, but are now "pale plump softness" concerned more with "parties" and "summer cottages" than the serious business of national defense, the "tight" "tracks of reality":

> As he sat talking with Dave, a preference for male companionship beat through him, surly, superior. Women talked of parties, of family, of children and summer cottages and love. This with Dave was what a man needed, this bone and muscle for the mind instead of pale plump softness. This men's talk was all in the hard clean outlines of battle, impossible bridges to be built

under fire, the split of the atom, the greed of looting armies. Dave had begun in Italy and gone through the whole business of D Day and the rest. He'd been wounded and mended and thrown back in. Women clawed softly at your manhood. War and work and the things you believed in gave it back to you. *This* gave it back to you, lounging in opposite chairs, taking the good short cuts men could take who'd been through the same things, fiddling through long drinks, arguing, differing or agreeing, but always tight on the tracks of reality. (129)

That men's empathy cannot be feminine or feminizing is made clear in two asides about gender identification. Early in his contemplation of difference and identification, Phil notes, "My trouble is . . . the only difference that rates with me is people's sex." Hobson goes on to describe Phil's reflection: "The notion amused him. 'I *do* care whether somebody's a man or a woman'" (47–48). At the book's end, the magazine staff wonders what Phil's next assignment will be. "'I was a woman for eight weeks?' Phil asked, and they all shouted" (268). The hilarity with which the staff greets this possibility (say, compared to the multiple *Quantum Leap* episodes where Sam actually does "land" in a woman's body) turns

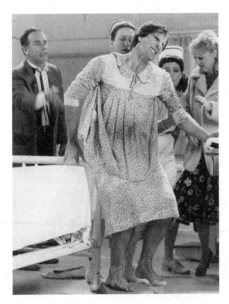

Figure 4. *Scientist Sam Beckett (Scott Bakula) "leaps" into the body and experience of a pregnant teenaged girl in episode 43 (1991) of the TV series* Quantum Leap.

a blind eye to the possibility of high heels as the next step in "walking in the other guy's shoes." But women are not a misunderstood or maltreated class, and women's particularity is too profound to be considered for appropriation by the universalized subjectivity under construction in the post–World War II period.[26]

The homopatriotic fusion of Phil and Dave masculinizes empathy as long as non-Zionist Jewishness is contained within America. With "over sensitiveness" attributed to the Jew (a patriot, an object of empathy, but not a citizen), with women ruled out as subjects for cross-identificatory empathy, the new citizen turns out to be a Christian, white, heterosexual, male.[27] Without explicitly being named, queerness is projected as the outer limit of mutual understanding. The admonitions against Zionism trace the edge of the alternate misalliance—to religion over nation.

Despite its surface discourse of personal attitude, anti-Semitism is approached from the perspective of nation rather than from the point of view of those subject to its devastation. Anti-Semitism is as dangerous as communism because it produces a Jewish identification—Zionism—which is in grave danger of pursuing another kind of world order. Anti-Semitism is both an individual threat and a force that can engender a response that runs against the most basic premise of modernity and its embodiment, America. The brilliant scientist Lieberman admonishes Phil to be discriminating in "experiencing" his brief Jewishness:

> Phil had defended "the Palestine solution" for the immediate present at least, [but] Lieberman's words came back to him. "Don't let them pull the crisis over your eyes. You say you oppose all nationalism—then how can you fall for a *religious* nationalism? A rejoining of church and state after all these centuries?" (212)

In the logical gambit to show how liberal pluralism can promote freedom while at the same time presuming the future of American dominance, we also learn how dangerous this new affectivity can be: the passing Christian may fail to recognize the heterogeneity in the particularity he has temporarily taken up. But since his "experience" will inevitably end—that is, after all, the comfort of both the Method and this new journalism, as opposed to, say, anthropology, where the practitioner may well "go native"—the Universal point of view will always recognize the central tendency in the American particulars that he might transiently occupy. Hiding America within the concept of freedom enables the production of a national identity that simultaneously transcends nation to speak of humanity and does so in the context of a community of nations, not world communism. The invocation of human rights is, always and simultaneously, a form of opposing particular figures of world order and allegiance beyond the nation: both the communist and the Zionist Jew.

Identity—the common referent of civil rights and human rights rhetoric—is the Rosemary's Baby of contemporary liberal pluralism. Born in a response to communism and installed at the heart of the identity politics it underwrites, identification in the forms imagined in the post–World War II era has a deep sympathy with a particular kind of national identity that preaches melodramatic empathy in place of a potentially erotic comradelove. With the empathetic citizen having absorbed much of what once marked suspect masculinities, the homosexual could figure empathy gone awry. The homosexual's crime was not so much feminization as the failure to make the turn from the strongest masculine identification of soldier toward an empathy that served the nation. Queerness is the collapse of political love into something else, a subterranean place in which goo leads not to transformation but fusion. Queerness is, in this instance, beyond—even against—identity. An antiqueer inscription of anticommunism lies at the heart of the political constellation that has produced contemporary gay politics.

Alienating Queer

Recounted by victims of the hearings who subsequently became gay activists, repeated in virtually every history gay Americans have written about ourselves, the activities of the HUAC provide a touchstone in gay countermemory, providing unity for an otherwise fragmentary politics. By creating an affective attachment to the very nation that has reviled us, the hagiographic incorporation of HUAC victims (and victimizers—the character of Roy Cohn works in *Angels in America* [Kushner 1995] because he signifies the complexities of queer unity for gay and lesbian activists) into our history helped secure our place as citizens. In articulating ourselves as unjustly deprived of civil rights in that moment, we participate in American citizenship, we respond to the desire for rights that will assimilate us to the whole of the nation. For many of us, that affective response has proved lifesaving. To the extent that it has succeeded, gay political efforts have convinced many—perhaps even a majority—of Americans that, as Newt Gingrich put it, most gay people are good citizens on most days. Maybe that is as much as we can get. Maybe it explains why we were offered a place, albeit it equivocally, in the military before we were given protection against discrimination under federal law.

Clearly much has changed in the constellation of alien, queer, and protected class, but their interconnection is only loosened, not rent. It may seem heartless to look beyond the stark evidence of blatant, vicious homophobia in the early cold war era, but revisiting this period with postidentitarian eyes has practical consequences for the queer politics framed around disrupting or taking over the idea of nationness. If nothing else, a more sanguine appreciation for the complex interrelationship of emotion and anticommunism provides a means to disrupt the easy accusation, only latent in some responses to Roy Cohn's character, that neither AIDS nor HUAC counts as oppression because "we," or the loose cannons "among us," brought these disasters upon ourselves. Even better, if in-your-face politics can recognize that the term under assault (citizenship?) and the idea under erasure (nation) are themselves already multiple and labile, then queer politics are not exclusively cultural but should go to the heart of definitions of the citizen that are woven into concrete practices of the state.[28] I've made some guesses as to why communistic activity—even by natural-born citizens—was construed as treasonous while the homosexual's practice, although making him suspect as a citizen, did not alienate him from the nation. Perhaps we should imagine how a Queer Nation might prepare to expatriate itself, to become alien, as a means of substantially challenging the very idea of nation. Without truly putting one's American citizenship at risk, without seriously entertaining the consequences of becoming a person without a nation, Queer Nation, though it refuses to specify its rules of membership, continually collapses into the identity politics that are, I've suggested here, inextricably tied to American nationalism. When it operates above the threshold of citizenship, trading in its privileges instead of criticizing the fantasies of nation and of rights, queerness risks being just another label for a group that liberal pluralism can easily accommodate.[29] The discourse of identity that Hobson places in the mouth of the book's most secular Jew suggests a way to more fully activate the productive phrase "queer nation" in order to generate some friction when queer citizenship meets citizenship in America, and in order to "queer" the legal categories and models of nationality that still cut through the citizen-nation complex.

The stereotypical-looking but secular-thinking scientist of *Gentleman's Agreement* proposes a politic that must have seemed nearly incoherent in its day. As a totally nonreligious and noncultural Jew, he argues for queering the category "Jew" by claiming not to be what he "obviously" is in order to disrupt the claim that such a thing has a particular significance.

> "My crusade will have a certain charm," Lieberman continued now. "I will go forth and state flatly, 'I am not a Jew.'" He looked at Phil. "With this face that becomes not an evasion but a new principle. A scientific principle."

But this plan has a problem "Because this world still makes it an advantage not to be one. . . . Only if there were no anti-Semites could I do it" (Hobson 1946, 212–13). He cannot—or rather, Hobson cannot—imagine a way to succeed in this politic as long as such a refusal of an attributive identity could be misunderstood as an attempt to pass, thereby reinforcing the shackling identity by appearing to desire to evade it. For Hobson, this politics can only be successful when it is no longer necessary.

Then why even propose it? Hobson sensed the possibilities of this strange space of attributive identity and passing, even though she couldn't quite work them out. In fact, it is the invisible queer, from a rather different vantage point, who may be able to make use of the strange lever she locates. Lieberman's plan is to doggedly avoid the reverse discourse, like that of the slogan "Gay is good," to step away from a debate of the relative advantages and disadvantages of particular social locations. He hints that we need to mobilize the perverse side of cross-identification and "natural" political love—his scheme has "an innocence—no, a sort of purity" (213)—that both invokes and dissembles in the face of the "grandeur from the degree to which [revolution] is felt to be something fundamentally pure" (Anderson 1991, 144). What Lieberman realizes is that face is less a mask, an obscuring addition, than it is a subtraction, a hole gouged out in the social landscape.

The seduction of identity is great, and the geophagia of the nation is terrifying. To be an effective new form of politics, queer must break from the legacy of nation that social movements have inherited. Queer must find a way to place its face outside nation, not, as some activists have urged, to shun the circulation of capital, but to refuse political love. A truly queer nation would offer habitation—a resting place for face—that one would not have to die for.

This nascent critique of the conditions that make passing political is spelled out more legibly in *Pinky*, a move that links identity and acting in a way that allows us to understand the political impact of social changes on the status of acting as such. Like *Gentleman's Agreement*, *Pinky* uses the device of a character who passes, but this time relies on the stock figure of the female mulatto who must make choices about her relationship with two worlds. Largely following the white "script" for such stories etched out in women's magazines of the inter- and postwar years, the film has received far less critical attention in recent years than the Douglas Sirk version of *Imitation of Life*. But more important than that banal plot is the critical response to *Pinky* in its day, and the fact that this wildly popular film was actually censored, a decision that eventually was appealed all the way to the U.S. Supreme Court, the very court that was considering the school desegregation case, *Brown v. Board of Education*.

3

CENSORSHIP AND THE PROBLEM FILMS

Censoring Race

E lia Kazan's *Pinky* opened in New York City in October 1949. Predictions that it would be one of the best-attended films of the year proved true. With box office receipts topping $4 million, *Pinky* was the fourth-biggest-grossing film that year and its three lead actresses each garnered an Academy Award nomination (Winnington 1976). The plot concerns a light-skinned Black woman, Pinky Johnson (played by white actress Jeanne Crain), who has been passing as white in the North while attending nursing school. She has fallen in love with an "unsuspecting" white doctor and, at the beginning of the film, returns to her grandmother's (Ethel Waters) home in the South to grapple with her intractable problem. When the white matriarch, Miss Em (Ethel Barrymore), who employs Pinky's grandmother falls ill, Pinky assumes the role of nurse and cares for her. Pinky and Miss Em develop a mutual respect, and when the old woman eventually dies, she wills Pinky her decaying plantation. After a court battle with Miss Em's relatives, Pinky's title to the property is secured. When Dr. Thomas Adams, her white Yankee fiancé, learns of Pinky's racial heritage, he assumes she has fought for the property on principle and will simply sell it and return to her "white" life. He

Figure 5. *Promotional posters marketed* Pinky *(1949) to a female audience primed for racial passing stories by popular magazines of the day.*

assures her that after they marry there will "be no more Pinky Johnson." But Pinky rejects their love and remains in the South where she turns the mansion into a training facility for Black nurses and a clinic for her "community."[1]

Pinky, which counterpoises the "temptation" to pass for the sake of unrecognized interracial love with an obligation to racial solidarity and community of origin, was censored as "prejudicial to the best interest of the people of" Marshall, Texas. The powers-that-be in that community felt the film would ignite racial conflict. This censoring was appealed to the Texas Court of Appeals, where it was upheld. In the end, it took the U.S. Supreme Court to overturn *Pinky*'s censorship. In 1952, the film joined the case concerning *The Miracle* (Roberto Rossellini, 1948) to inaugurate a decade-long dismantling of the rationales for state-initiated censorship of representations other than the most definitively obscene. In its back-to-back decisions regarding *The Miracle* and *Pinky,* the Supreme Court struck down its own 1915 decision (in *Mutual Film Corp. v. Industrial Commission of Ohio* [236 U.S. 230, 1915], hereafter *Mutual*) that movies were not subject to either First or Fourteenth Amendment protection; in the new thinking, censorship provisions against *The Miracle* and *Pinky* (concerning sacrilege and racial representations, respectively) were pronounced vague and thereby unconstitutional. To enact this change of heart, the Supreme Court struck down the state-level ruling against *The Miracle,* a case called *Joseph Burstyn, Inc. v. Wilson, Commissioner of New York, et al.* (Appeal from Court of Appeals of New York, No. 522, 343 U.S. 495, 1952, hereafter *Burstyn*) and argued at length that the film, though perhaps offensive to Catholics, was part of a debate about, not an impermissible attack on, religion. Similarly, in their decision in the *W. L. Gelling v. State of Texas* case (343 U.S. 960, 1952, hereafter *Gelling*) *Pinky,* seized under a law designed to prevent showing of films that might incite racial violence, was considered by the court to be part of the debate about America's social ills, a vehicle for discussing the "Negro problem," not a potential source of racial conflict. *Gelling* was thus overturned and race-related prohibitions struck down.

Of the many censored films[2] that might have been used as test cases, *The Miracle* and *Pinky* have special social significance as the occasion for striking down the Supreme Court's 1915 decision in *Mutual,* which had declared movies entertainment, not vehicles of protected speech. In taking on *The Miracle,* the Court seemed to be saying that activist Catholics, perhaps the single largest force in shaping film censorship practices, would no longer be such major players in determining what the American public would see. In overturning *Pinky*'s censoring without arguing the case in detail, the Court suggested that racism should be discussed openly, even if the Court would not participate in the discussion. The cultural firestorm that began with D. W. Griffith's *Birth of a Nation* (*Mutual* was the decision that permitted its censoring) was nearing its end; "serious" films were no longer considered coercive promoters of ideas, but the site or vehicle for popular debate about *social* issues.

In short, a lot had changed between 1915 and 1952. In the first moment, movies were considered so dangerous they could cause race riots or tear a nation apart through a kind of cultural civil war. By the time *Mutual* was struck down, movies were important to America's growing understanding of religious and racial prejudice. How was the visual sign converted from a vehicle for destructive, ominous effects to a productive source of multiple interpretation? Was this just another example of the liberalizing of American attitudes? Another step in the long march forward toward an enlightened society? The court cases mark a change, but they do not fully explain what changed or how one interpretive logic unraveled and a second emerged. As I have been arguing throughout this book, important aspects of the subjectivity of the citizen were under pressure in the post–World War II era. Here I want to suggest that a new semiotic regime, which yoked a psychology to a semiology and an acting style, was consolidated in the late 1940s in tandem with the need to constitute the new subjectivity discussed in the previous chapters. This reconfiguration of art, law, and citizenship afforded movies a central role in American society.

As with the immigration laws I reviewed in chapter 2, I will suggest here with regard to censorship that the proscription of certain images of the Black body were complexly related to narratives of proscribed sexuality. However, as I also warned earlier, we cannot simply interchange signs of race and of sexuality; we cannot suggest that one is "really about" the other. Rather, the signs of race and of sexuality operate in different semiotic registers, so that crafters and dismantlers of film censorship codes had to struggle, over the course of the first half of the twentieth century, to construct a psychology that would explain why particular signs acted on the viewer in one way or another. For example, when the courts "read" the blackfaced body in *The Birth of a Nation*, they saw a sign whose iconic and indexical dimensions multiplied each other's intensity; these body images invoked a powerful, almost intolerable, national memory of racist prohibition and white violence. However, when the Black body was read as a sign in which the different registers of signification operate separately—that is, when they were split signs of the type we will encounter when I return to analyze the U.S. Supreme Court's decision regarding *Pinky*—the Black body's indexing of *racism* could override the dangerous connotative associations of its iconic role as a desired or desiring body.

But how is it possible to write a genealogy of a visual sign? Isn't the history of censorship a history of proscribed signs? Perhaps. Those interested in film will have noticed that while both historians and textual critics have spilled much ink on the subject of American films of the classic period—roughly coextensive with the regime of legal and industry-imposed censorship—there has been little simultaneous attention to the historical situation *and* formal properties of particular films. Censorship historiography, focused as it is on the legal and social mechanisms of prohibition, provides no easy route into treatment of film *form,* since film form requires a theory of interpretation, itself dependent on some kind of psychology of sign perception. Textual criticism has, in waves, canonized films and then valorized the symptomatically ignored films. By chance or because of the films' treatment as the objects of censorship scholars' histories, formal discussions of film rarely embrace as textually significant the films that were the object of legal debate. Generally speaking, explanations of changing censorship practices have underplayed the changes in film aesthetics and film interpretation, while academic critics have appeared loathe to analyze the censored films as formal objects.

But it seems to be the case that the popular sense that the signs are polyvalent emerged simultaneously with the film industry's new concern with "prejudice." Particular images of the Black body, which had once been so dangerous they had to be suppressed, became a means to signify white racism. The end of official, racially based censorship was simultaneous with the inauguration of a new meaning for the Black body in film. However, the end of race-based prohibitions in the 1950s did not liberate the sexual-racial history on which the meaning and censorship of Black body/images had depended. Instead, it repressed that history by representing the experience of racial oppression to a white audience as a social "problem." The industry's censorship code and the law had once prohibited images of Black bodies that whites might find threatening. But the newly emergent images, while contested by segregationists, had somehow lost their threatening quality. This was not because white Americans were more tolerant, but because the Black body of the postcensorship decade of problem films still did not refer to actual Black people. Rather, it indexed the idea of racism, an idea that white Americans could discuss because racists could now be specified as Southern and/or archaic.

There are several problems in trying to understand the specific institutional and social practices surrounding raced signs. First, the genealogy of signs from different semiogenic domains cannot be read as a unified history of permission/prohibition. Courts and filmmakers collide in an event like *Pinky*'s censorship; the techniques, theories, and institutional support of sign interpretation are asymmetrical, and the changes that occur within the domains of art and law are quite different. For example, art tends to operate through aesthetic breaks and explicit re-theorization of the perceptual, while the law means contending with precedent: changing the law requires logical extension rather than aesthetic break. To further complicate a unified history, there were actually very few active film censorship boards, and each operated under different statutes, some completely out of touch with the changing industry Code, which, in turn, had no legal enforcement mechanism.[3] Although there was an uneven, indirect relationship between the individual censorship boards and the increasingly elaborate Code, the courts had no legal oversight of the essentially private self-regulation of the film industry and could only act upon the narrowly worded statutes that the Supreme Court ultimately struck down.

The passage of nearly thirty-seven years between the establishment of legal censorship and its curtailment means that the 1915 support for *Mutual* and the 1952 *Burstyn* and *Gelling* reversals stand as bookends to the more complex set of changes in ideas about the moving image; the shifts in the industry Code represented in detail a rupture in interpretive logic that would, in the end, make most film censorship untenable. Holding in tension the difference between municipal censorship bodies, and their regulation through the court cases discussed here, and the versions of the industry's own codes as it negotiated the moral economy of its product, I will nevertheless read theses two interests—state and industry—against each other to tease out what they together suggest about the changing popular understandings of what filmic signs are and do.

Cinematic Prohibition

D. W. Griffith's *Birth of a Nation* occasioned the signal case that served as the legal precedent for state censorship of film for thirty-seven years. The popular debate about the film centered on its interpretation of race relations in the postbellum South: the NAACP protested the film's depiction of Blacks; then-President Woodrow Wilson praised it as if the film laid bare America's racist legacy. But the legal debate followed a different trajectory and began when the company that was distributing *The Birth of a Nation,* Mutual Film Corp., challenged the Ohio state board of censors' licensing requirement that all films shown in the state be subject to its scrutiny. Mutual wanted an injunction to stop the board from exercising its power, arguing that it cost too much money to ship films for review and that, more importantly, the board was unfairly curbing First Amendment rights. The board, meanwhile, threatened to arrest anyone who would show a film in Ohio that it had not first approved. In 1915, the U.S. Supreme Court heard the case. In essence, the judges were given the task of determining the status of moving image signs: did they, like newspapers or radio, convey information (and therefore earn First Amendment protection), or, like the circus, merely evoke feelings? In his 1915 pamphlet, "The Rise and Fall of Free Speech in America" (see Mast 1982, 321–33), director Griffith argued that film deserved protection from censorship not because it functioned like a newspaper, but because it functioned differently: movies had a formally specific way of representing history. Using an established logic that film produced effects more "memorable" than other media (58–61), Griffith argued that *The Birth of a Nation* embodied "truth" not because the images it deployed were real in themselves, but because the moral that movies invoked made history real to the masses:

> Fortunes are spent every year in our country in teaching the truths of history, that we may learn from the mistakes of the past. . . . The truths of history today are restricted to the limited few attending our colleges and universities; the motion picture can carry these truths to the entire world, without cost, while at the same time bring diversion to the masses. (133)

Griffith recognized that there were differences between his historical movies and the simultaneously emergent documentary form; it was the combination of historical reference and diversion that promised that fictional film as a medium could change the world.

> As tolerance would thus be compelled to give way before knowledge as the deadly monotony of the cheerless existence of millions would be brightened by this new art, two of the chief causes making war possible would be removed. The motion picture is war's greatest antidote. (132)

Although he foregrounded the educational value of movies in order to argue for their right to First Amendment protection, by pinning his case to the dual nature of film—referential *and* pleasurable—Griffith equivocated on precisely the issue the court needed to rule on. The controversy surrounding the film's accuracy and political intent may have influenced the court's decision to uphold censorship generally: it was easier to declare film incapable of truth than to adjudicate the truth of America's racial history. Nevertheless, the court declared even partially nonfiction works—the enormously popular historical, biographical, and gangster films (the first "issue" films)—to be entertainment, subject to "taste" but not "truth."

Although the suppression of *The Birth of a Nation* may have seemed like a small victory for those struggling against racism, the Court did not directly base its findings on the issue of misrepresentation. *The Birth of a Nation* was censored not because it was racist, but because stereotypical representations of Blacks (albeit, played by blackfaced white actors) attempting to rape white women or engaging in violent revolt were perceived as capable of inciting Black viewers to criminal behavior; it was censored not because it was unacceptable to be "entertained" at the expense of another group, but because the "attractiveness and manner of exhibition" made film reception potentially more dangerous than newspaper or pamphlet reception (Mast 1982, 142). The First Amendment logic of the time argued that the statement of opinions should be unrestrained, but it also held individuals liable for their behavior if they acted on their opinions in a criminal manner. Film was different: its mass reception and viscerally evocative power meant that it engendered a *collective* response that might exceed the capacity to police the resultant actions. Critically, this was the logic that had secured the legal principle of "separate but equal" in the 1896 Supreme Court case *Plessy v. Ferguson* (163 U.S. 537, 1896, hereafter *Plessy*), regarding racial segregation of public transportation. The wording of the decision is particularly important in understanding the covert legal logic of the *Mutual* decision. In *Plessy*, the Court, opposing the concepts of equality and liberty, argued that liberty supersedes all but the most minimal right to legal equality. The Court accomplished this revaluation of basic constitutional principles by splitting *social* equality (a concept that would haunt the quest for Black civil rights by suggesting that such equality would include miscegenation [see Cayton and Drake 1945]) from *legal* equality, narrowing the scope of the emancipation-related constitutional amendments and ending the Radical Reconstructionists' use of the high court to pursue change at the state level. Most importantly, the Court reframed the due process clause to invent municipalities as entities to be legally protected: the unpredictable (but presumptively violent) consequences of social mixing of the races imposed a requirement on a town to maintain the peace that it might be unable to fulfill. Forced integration was argued as violating the due process rights of a town because it did not have an opportunity to make a case for why its system of racial segregation was not already a fulfillment of the legal minimum.

Although the *Mutual* decision concerning the fate of *The Birth of a Nation* does not explicitly spell out this logic, the Court relied on the presumption about the potentially violent consequences of "social" relations between Blacks and whites when it allowed censors to act in cases where a film might be, as the *Gelling* decision would state, "prejudicial to the interests of" a town. In retrospect, it is clear that *The Birth of a Nation* was censored not because its sign-images failed their referent ("history"), but because movies were understood to be interpreted corporally, not cognitively: movies were feeling, not speech. This newly articulated theory of media effects underwrote the Court's decision, which dealt with the anxiety over the volatility of racial mixing by banning particular forms of racial representation whose effects, like "fighting words," were less easy to contain than the separate but equal social partition could guarantee. Thus, the "truth" at risk in *The Birth of a Nation* was not the film's lack of fidelity to a history America wanted to claim, but its connection to a present that progressive America preferred to ignore—the post-Reconstructionist white terrorism that resulted in lynching of Black men well into the twentieth century. *The Birth of a Nation's* lack of historical accuracy was directly proportional to its unconscious truth: far more white Americans continued to hold racist beliefs—and might be incited to act on them—than anyone wanted to admit. As Blacks at the time feared, it was white rage and not Black criminality that the film threatened to unleash. But where the language of prejudiciality had a clear social referent in the teens—representation of unnamable things that drove white men crazy—the emerging movie industry's self-censorship was quite explicit in detailing the raced image that was to be banned: "miscegenation."

Race Mixing

Unlike the legal double speak of prejudiciality, which linked intimations of cross-race relations to the post-Reconstructionists' interpretation of the Fourteenth Amendment, the charge of "miscegenation" was quite clear: film censors' were frank about their unhappiness about race mixing and about their concern with a specific form of sexual desire—that between the "black and white races." But it would be overly simplistic to view the codes as solely affirmatively racist, since they are also racist by complicity with unspoken ideas about race relations. White antagonism toward the miscegenators clearly had immediate, violent consequences, but it is hard to make good on the claim that film censorship aimed to protect such couples. Indeed, "miscegenation" was discussed in code restrictions related to sexuality, not to the violence that the law presumed would ensue. (As I will show below, by the 1930s censors had rather different worries about the harms of sexual versus violent images: representation of perversions was thought to ignite sexual desires, not violent revenge.) White antagonism toward miscegenation was actually part of a much more complex attempt to repress a specific history of systematic and double denial of Black women's agency, both the literal denial of her agency when raped or coerced, and the denial of her agency when she dangerously and subversively willed her sexuality across the racial divide.[4] But while prejudiciality stands along with the white terrorism that *Plessy* pretended to want to avoid, the code's proscription of miscegenation attempts to forestall white men's attraction to Black women in the first instance. In prewar years, as the code developed, there may have been two sides to this coin—the representation of Black men and white women was the source of violent retribution, while the fact of white men's ongoing abuse of Black women was tolerated, but not promoted. It is important to note that even so clear a prohibition is confused about *how* racial signs make meaning: the code provides no rationale for banning the mixed-race couple while at the same time allowing producers to opulently utilize the "mulatto," who was represented as an off-screen mixed-race couple's tragic issue.

Though it seems obvious to whom the early codes were referring, the prohibition was never explicitly stated. In 1930, however, the Hays Code specifically defined miscegenation as "sex relationships between the white and black races." Indeed, a variety of other cross-racial and cross-ethnic relationships were part of the iconography and symbolism of film: relationships between Anglos and Asians or Anglos and Native Americans were never proscribed, and no films were ever censored for representing other interracial or interethnic relations.

In fact, in Westerns, race and ethnicity operated as signs that only secondarily made reference to the race of the persons who carried racial markers: whole plots, and the larger contemplation of the moral logic of civilization, relied on the shorthand system signified through varying combinations of Anglo-Native sexual relationships. The social conflicts of star-crossed lovers (almost always Anglo men and Native or mixed women) and the internal conflicts of the "half-breed" (usually male and the incontrovertible evidence of the sexuality of an earlier Anglo-Native union) each symbolized the problems of a rapidly developing United States. Varying combinations—actually, a complex calculus—of mixed and unmixed males from multiple generations provided gradations of conflict between forms of masculinity, all at play on a feminine, if often not virgin, body/landscape. Situated in/as the native land, the Native woman is barred from going to the city; often she dies, or is the pathetic symbol of what must be left behind.

In their iconic aspect, women "half-breeds" were represented as doubly fallen: fallen from the Native way and fallen as the product of rape by "bad" soldiers or bandits of any of several ethnicities. Significantly, the rape scenes were quite clearly invoked, but not in order to condemn the acts of violence against Native women, but rather because they provided the opportunity to exonerate the "good" white men who chased bandits and show the impotence of Native men, who were powerless to stop the theft of their land and women, transformed through the capitalist logic of most Westerns into forms of property, not elements of an integrated way of life. (And thus, the Western denies that in "saving" the Native women, the white hero is also destroying entire families and cultures.)

Anglo-Asian relations have also been crucial in framing plots about the decay of Anglo social relations. At first, Asian men symbolized drug and alcohol abuse, but beginning in the interwar years, Asian women began to suggest the susceptibility of Anglo men to the *most* feminine sexuality, which rubs off and demasculinizes them. The most famous of this earlier type is Griffith's apologetic, post–*Birth of a Nation* plea for racial tolerance, *Broken Blossoms* (1919). The many versions of the Mata Hari story, in which an inventive female spy gains access to military/state secrets through seduction, are examples of the latter.

While Mexicans in particular did not fare well in Hollywood's utilization of raced signs to convey abstract concepts and compressed narratives, Anglo-Latino/a relations in general were not considered miscegenating. As United States–Latin geopolitical relations evolved through the twentieth century, Latin American characters occupied a variety of stereotypical positions in film. Sexual attraction to or rejection of Latinos/as encoded class distinction as much as ethnic differences: Latinos/as seem not to have been considered a different race. (Cuban) Ricky and (redheaded) Lucy Ricardo could invade our homes without a hint of inappropriate racial mixing.

There were two forms of restriction on Black-white sexual representations that were highly specific to the historical situation of the post-Reconstruction era, two specific logics that did not apply to other races, however much they were considered inferior or inappropriate love objects for whites. The law traced a growing trend toward recuperating segregation by asserting the implacability of violent outcomes of literal co-presence of the races in a common space. Meanwhile, the film codes set limitations based on ideas about visual perceptions that might stir sexual desires.

From Image to Story

Debate about what was acceptable content for movies began with the first public exhibitions of the emergent medium. In the first two decades of the twentieth century, many municipalities and several states crafted censorship statutes, many modeled after one produced by the National Board of Censorship (renamed the National Board of Review in 1922), an industry-sympathetic board formed in 1909 in conjunction with the People's Institute of New York. Designed to forestall state control and reacting to antimovie activism by women's clubs and Catholic Church groups, the board recruited a range of "civic-minded" volunteers to review and recommend "acceptable" films to states or municipalities (Mast 1982, 60). Experience might have brought clarity and consistency to the board's practices, but censors found it increasingly difficult to decide what to suppress. In 1921, the National Board of Censorship reviewers argued against legal censorship, specifically due to the lack of consistency among individual censors, local differences in censorship concerns, and the lack of a central rationale for nationwide censorship (191–94). At the same moment that censors were discovering the textual indeterminacy of film and debates about film's moral value were reaching a fever pitch, the industry was changing: growing rapidly, experimenting wildly (sound and color were introduced in the 1920s), professionalizing, and facing charges of monopolizing. Industry self-policing was increasingly difficult.[5] In 1926, the Motion Picture Producers and Distributors Association of America (MPPDA) established a department of studio relations that was to mediate between the studios and the most active local and state censors. For nearly two years, the director of the new office met with producers to review scripts and films and to suggest—apparently with considerable accuracy—changes likely to meet activists' and official censors' approval (de Grazia and Newman 1982, 30). In late 1927, the department released a list of "do's and don'ts" based on the previous year and a half of experience.

This first film code produced by the industry as an industry was a list presumed to correspond exactly to the visual signs to be prohibited in movies:

> . . . produced by members of this association, irrespective of the manner in which they are treated: pointed profanity; any licentious or suggestive nudity—in fact or in silhouette; the illegal traffic in drugs; any inference of sex perversion; white slavery; miscegenation; sex hygiene and venereal diseases; scenes of actual childbirth—in fact or in silhouette; children's sex organs; ridicule of the clergy; willful offense to any nation, race, or creed. (Mast 1982, 213–14)

Despite the 1915 Supreme Court ruling that excluded film from First Amendment protection, the legal finding that film was "entertainment" and not information did not sufficiently justify all the provisions crusaders wanted in the code. Ambivalence about censorship in general—and the difficulty of specifying what images were acceptable and why—forced the MPPDA to provide an increasingly complex specification of prohibitions and justifications for voluntarily undertaking self-regulation. Never legitimated by law, the code not only had to describe what to prohibit from film but also to address challenges to its administrator's authority to provide such guidelines. In 1930, the MPPDA assembled conservative ideas about the meaning and social role of movies and produced the famous Hays Code, which differed from its predecessor in two ways: it included an extensive rationale for industry self-policing and offered a new means of categorizing what was to be prohibited from movies. Together these changes revealed a shift in the relative value of image versus plot as the source of films' meaning.

Since it was not legally binding but could only try to preempt legal entanglement, the new code contained a logic for predicting what might be censored. Recognizing the religious commitments of Catholic antimovie activists, and cognizant of its tenuous legal position, the MMPDA crafted the Hays Code by welding theological justifications to natural rights ideals to justify the proposed restrictions. Far removed from the debates about free speech, the code argued that film could be a force for good in society, but *as* entertainment, not as information. In one breath, the code accepted the general outline of the Supreme Court's *Mutual* decision—that film was not information—but constructed a moral role for film that was even more high-minded than Griffith's claim of film's capacity to popularize history. Film might not be "information," but

> . . . entertainment can be of a character harmful to the human race, and in consequence [society] has clearly distinguished between:
>
> a. Entertainment which tends to improve the race, or at least to recreate and rebuild human beings exhausted with the realities of life; and
>
> b. Entertainment which tends to degrade human beings, or to lower their standards of life and living. (Mast 1982, 321)

The industry's ambition was to provide the former, while dissociating itself from illegitimate works in celluloid that accomplished the latter. But the values of rejuvenation versus degradation were not exactly mirror opposites since one could, presumably, be "exhausted with the realities of life" without being degraded. The asymmetrical difference was secured by distinguishing between the two forms of an image's violation: the distinction between natural versus human law, mentioned in passing in the code, is elaborated in the longer "Reasons" version (320):

> . . . By natural law is understood the law which is written in the hearts of all mankind, the great underlying principles of right and justice dictated by conscience. By human law is understood the law written by civilized nations.

This split also underwrote the code's distinction between sex and criminality/violence, which may each "degrade," but through violation of natural versus human law. The distinction between crimes against nature and crimes against the law influenced the different ways producers were to handle sex versus violence: "sex" merited its own category in the Hays Code, while "violence" was proscribed under provisions dealing with "crimes against the law." The code's division between content (literally, the images) and style ("vulgarity and suggestiveness" versus "good taste") overlapped closely, but imprecisely, with the violence-sex distinction. Advice on "taste" (plotting of stories of love or crime, but also use of dancing, sexually evocative locations, and ridicule of religions) was offered separately from sections prohibiting particular images (which included crime and the outer reaches of sex-related images—"perversion" and "miscegenation" among them). But images and plots were not so easily separated, resulting in considerable repetition among sections in the code: censors did not yet have a theory of the sign that hypothesized aspects (essence/accident, icon, index, symbol, etc.) that could explain how a single image might operate in multiple, even contradictory ways.

Two different rationales for censoring were necessary because interpretation of and response to images tended in two directions: natural and social or human. For the code's writers, representation of "crimes against the law" caused imitation, while representations of "sex"—implicitly, crimes against natural law but explicitly, images that might disrupt the "sanctity of the institution of marriage and the home" (332)—decreased the inhibition to act on latent desires. Instead of interrogating properties of the sign to resolve the problems created by the lopsided polarities structured into the 1930 Code—natural versus human law, sex versus violence, proscribed versus plot-circumscribed—censors produced an equivalently unwieldy and dualistic theory of reception. The problem with criminality was that it put ideas into the viewer's head that might not otherwise be there. The problem with sexuality was that it was all *too* present, ready to boil over in almost any form. For example, "brutal killings" were to be minimized so that films would not be a "possible school in crime methods," and "the technique of murder [was to be] presented in a way that [would not] inspire imitation" by potential criminals (332). But where only certain people were inclined toward criminality, and then only once they learned the techniques to commit crimes, virtually everyone was susceptible to the arousal of their lustful emotions: "All legislators have recognized clearly that there are in normal human beings emotions which react naturally and spontaneously to the presentation of certain definite manifestations of sex and passion" (327). Thus, in the absence of either a clearly worked out theory of the sign, or a means of verifying the signs' proposed effects on an audience, the film code hovered between a theory of perception and a psychology: the code could not decide whether the potential harm of film resided in what and how viewers *saw* or in which emotions and sensations were aroused. This uncertainty, and the repetitions in the code that suggested that some images were problematic both *as* images and despite (or because) of their syntactic placement, made clear its authors' search for a logic of the sign as bi-morphic, that is as operating doubly in individual perception. But even a more complex theory of the sign could not explain why some audiences failed to "imitate" violent images or responded indifferently to steamy plots. A theory of audience was required.

The code suggested that not only did images operate in two modes—those that worked contextually were subject to taste while those that were somehow explicit, regardless of context, were to be banned outright—but there were also two different kinds of audiences: those who were unduly affected by films (children, the lower classes, and possibly women, and, at least in racial representations, Blacks) and those who were not affected (presumably

Figure 6. *The brutal scene of attempted rape in* Pinky *escaped censors' attention (Jeanne Crain with two uncredited actors), but not the amorous and supposedly cross-race interactions of its lead characters (Jeanne Crain and William Lundigan).*

middle-class white men). By the 1970s, psychoanalytic film theory and audience research treated the problems of differential reception by "subject" position or by "community," and the differential operation of signs (eventually dubbed polysemy) within film as separate issues. But the Hays Code melded biological theories of film perception with class distinctions and aligned these concerns under a single rationale for industry self-censorship. This cast a *particular* kind of audience as especially susceptible to both sex and violence. The reception theory proposed by the code assumed that by acting on the soul through the eye, the flickering image was particularly capable of triggering unconscious feelings and desires; film could arouse "dangerous emotions" in the "immature, young, and criminal classes." Even innocuous images were capable of taking on perverse meanings for some audiences. Image-plot combinations were unpredictable: not only were images of perversions to be eliminated, but love plots of a non-perverse nature had to be carefully handled as well. The 1930 code attempted to cope with the destabilization of a simple theory of the image and its effect by crafting a new theory, which, though more elaborate, rested on asymmetrical polarities that were even less adjudicable as guidelines for film composition. In particular, the kiss was a sign whose function was difficult to pin down. Indeed, in the case of *Pinky*, what seems to have provoked the censor's ire was not the scene of attempted rape (which was much more explicit and protracted than the code suggested was necessary to a plot), but a series of kisses between the protagonist (played by the then-well-known Jeanne Crain) and her lesser-known leading man (William Lundigan).

When a Kiss Is Not a Kiss

Film kisses have had a complicated history, precisely contingent on the uneasy fusion of documentarity (the profilmic event directly recorded) and narrative (the deployment of images to create a story) in the representational theories of film producers, viewers, and critics. As a significantly commercial medium—as entertainment rather than art—movies have been influenced from the start in content and style by what audiences liked and did not like. There was by no means a straight line between producers and consumers; audiences for film came from a range of consumption cultures, and the degree to which individual producers actually adjusted works to perceived audience preferences varied. Nevertheless, it is clear that one of the earliest Edison films (in fact, one of a triad often described as the beginning of American film) was quite negatively received, apparently evoking physical discomfort and moral outrage in the audience. The brief 1896 film *The Kiss*, virtually documentary footage of May Irwin and John Rice engaging in the eponymous act, produced a riot. Subsequent attempts to outline acceptable images grappled with the strange evocative power of this cinematic kiss.

As the codes evolved, it became apparent that the white, heterosexual kiss is another split sign that operates visually as an iconic (an actual kiss) or indexical (an act essentially linked to sexual desire) sign, but *narratively* as a symbol: love completed or achieved, love about to be betrayed, true love, first love. The task faced by compliant producers was to avail themselves of the economy various kisses offered to the narrative without slipping into the sign's dangerous iconic or indexical aspects. The issue for cinema-goers then was to correctly interpret the meaning of a kiss—or, perversely, to overread it—in the context of the film. This was a clever game that may well have formed invisible sub-hermeneutics; as Vito Russo (1981) has shown, male-male kisses have often occurred as part of humorous plot twists. These kisses were not explicitly indexical—that is, they did not mean to indicate the homosexual desire of the represented characters—but iconic, literally representing an event that will elicit the disgust of the actors once they recognize what they have done. To the extent that an aspect of the sign implies imminent sex, the visual "accident," which recruits the male-male kiss as a symbol of the failure to look before pursing, overrides the iconic and indexical aspects: as a composite sign, the play of sign moments also makes light of the incapacity of kissing to completely convey sex—male or female—and heterosexuality. Thus, the male-male kiss operates as a visual parody on sexuality's semiotic status in an intensely scopic economy: the very element that makes the kiss *romantic* (keeping your eyes closed) creates the danger of sex (or race) misrecognition. The participants cannot insure heterosexuality without "peeking," but that diminishes eroticism. The viewer is required to be both a voyeur—a pervert—and also the witness to heterosexuality. At the moment of the queer kiss, the actors act a recognition that "something is wrong," but what? The fact of two men, or that the kiss cannot produce the sexual closure it is assigned in the narrative? The mirroring of two physiognomies (shot-reverse-shot seems designed for this kind of instability!) reinstitutes the sex difference. The kiss, as an interconnection of identical—"homo"—bodily parts, is intrinsically incapable of conveying the very heterosexuality it symbolizes unless the bodies connected to the lips are already clearly sex-differentiated. The homosexual "mistake" forces the bodies apart with gestures of disgust; ironically, like the same-race, cross-sex kiss, it ultimately conveys heterosexuality.

But if same-sex kissing was, when recuperated, funny, cross-race kissing was deadly. The rare cross-race kisses that caused both *Pinky* and *Native Son* to be censored joined two once-separate regimes of acting; by iconizing the Black body first, race-*mixing* is no longer indexed (and sublated) but becomes iconic. If, ironically, homosexuality is completely banished once the "mistake" of sameness is discovered, the discovery of misrecognized race places cross-race desire within heterosexuality, but provides no shore of "otherness" at which heterosexuality might anchor its monochromicity. The 1965 Sidney Poitier film *A Patch of Blue* plays with the recuperability of the cross-race kiss: because the white protagonist is literally blind, she cannot "see" the reflection of her racial difference from the Black protagonist.

Censoring *Pinky*

Assessing the undoing of *Pinky*'s censorship is difficult given that the Supreme Court's judgment ran a scant single page. But its very brevity was symptomatic of both the Court's willingness to strike down race-related provisions and its anxiety about dealing head-on with the racial dimension of the representation of sexuality. As mentioned earlier, the cases involving *Pinky*, a Hollywood production, and *The Miracle,* an Italian art film that had deeply offended Catholics (Walters 1952), were both heard in 1952. In retrospect, *Pinky* should have been the precedent-setting decision; the film was, after all, censored for the same reasons as *The Birth of a Nation* and, as such, it was the more economical challenge to existing law. Indeed, the movie industry, which had been trying since 1915 to avoid legal censorship of films, hoped that the case to end all cases would be a homegrown box office favorite. It was in the industry's interest to tie both films to the issue of producers' freedom of expression rather than raising the thorny issue of freedom to occupy social and representational spaces (which had been the subtle but key legal logic in the *Mutual* case). The Supreme Court, which also had the historic *Brown v. Board of Education* case on its docket,[6] might itself have preferred to hear *Pinky* in order to strengthen its eventual reversal of *Plessy,* which, as I have noted, is the ghost behind the *Mutual* case. But at the same time, the municipal censorship regulations that had been used to censor *Pinky* were themselves very brief when compared to the New York regulations, which the industry's own code had often mirrored. Thus, while *Pinky* arrived at the Supreme Court first, the justices declined to consider the case until they'd heard *Burstyn,* the case in which *The Miracle* was censored as sacrilegious in the state of New York.[7]

The Supreme Court decision to hear *Burstyn* first had important repercussions, since *the* precedent-setting case would concern "sacrilege" rather than "prejudiciality." In its decision, the Supreme Court reversed the New York state-level decision that had upheld censorship of *The Miracle* and specifically attacked the state's citation of *Mutual* in its decision.

The judges in *Burstyn* find particularly problematic the following claim in the *Mutual* case:

> It cannot be put out of view that the exhibition of moving pictures is a business pure and simple, originated and conducted for profit, like other spectacles, not to be regarded, nor intended to be regarded by the Ohio constitution, we think, as part of the press of the country or as organs of public opinion. (500)

The Supreme Court in *Burstyn* reversed this opinion completely. As Mr. Justice Clark put it in his written judgment:

> It cannot be doubted that motion pictures are a significant medium for the communication of ideas. They may affect public attitudes and behavior in a variety of ways, ranging from direct espousal of a political or social doctrine to the subtle shaping of thought which characterizes all artistic expression. The importance of motion pictures as an organ of public opinion is not lessened by the fact that they are designed to entertain as well as to inform. (501)

With *Burstyn* as the new precedent then, the Court chose to focus attention on First rather than Fourteenth Amendment issues—

film was no longer mere entertainment but rather part of the class of material occupied by printed fiction and news, limitations on which were being challenged elsewhere at the same time. The re-classification of film was significant in two ways: first, by moving film into another area of well-defined case law, reclassification decreased the need to pursue high court decisions specific to film; but second, and perhaps more subtly, reclassification denied that the medium, a combination of image and sound, was in any important way different from print, photography, sound, or moving image alone. Having emerged from the debased category of entertainment, the movies found themselves an also-ran in First Amendment case law and legally indistinguishable from other organs of free speech.

The Supreme Court's decision represented a significant departure from the 1930 Hays Code's psycho-physiological concept of film interpretation, morally grounded as it was in crypto-Catholicism and abstract platitudes about human rejuvenation through entertainment. Instead, the Court suggested that film meaning was by nature hard to secure; it was part of, not a distraction from, the social and political process of coming to terms with a pluralist society. Justice Clark's majority opinion cited the just-decided *Winters v. New York* case (333 U.S. 507, 1948), which had revolved around criminalizing publication or distribution of violent or graphic printed material (essentially pulp fiction and sensational tabloid material popular during the Great Depression and after), recalling that in that case, the state court had held that:

> The line between the informing and the entertaining is too elusive for the protection of that basic right [a free press]. Everyone is familiar with instances of propaganda through fiction. What is one man's amusement, teaches another's doctrine. (*Winters* quoted in *Burstyn*, 501)

The Supreme Court thus entered the debates about contemporary politics and about the medium itself via *Burstyn* and even considered and cited reviews of, and letters about, *The Miracle* as part of its legal opinion. Not constraining himself to the level of legal citation, Justice Frankfurter,[8] in his concurring opinion, extensively cited newspaper and magazine reviews as if they were privileged evaluations of the truth of *The Miracle,* worthy to be introduced as part of a major legal opinion. This secondary use of critical material allowed him to differentiate his activity (objective legal judgment) from that of the censors, represented as strange, prudish voyeurs who were preventing *us* from seeing the lurid things they got to see. Declining to make his own reading of the film (it is not clear from the opinion whether or not he had seen it), Frankfurter used the reviewers' various opinions as evidence for diversity of reception, which he held as essential to American democracy—as opposed, say, to the perceived uniformity of communist or fascist aesthetic life.

Now assimilated to other forms of free speech about American social and political life, film became accepted as another medium through which to express political opinions; not a potential source of dangerous "propaganda," but a complex and multifaceted commentary that was to be received *as* political. Because it included so many different opinions about film in writing its own Opinion *of* film, the Court refused to act as censor. In constructing film as an intertext, the Court simultaneously demonstrated the polyvalence of moving images' popular reception and established audiences (and in some respects, I suppose, the market) rather than censors as the court of appeal regarding a film's meaning and value. As the principle vehicles for the Supreme Court reversals, problem films were doubly legitimated as a new genre; they were both the assertion of a political position and useful objects for popular debate. But this new availability of the medium of film as a space for political reflection complicated the meaning and level of the semiotics of both race and racism. If the Court's concern in *The Miracle* (i.e., *Burstyn*) was to open up the space for debate about morality (and not allow such debate to be deemed an attack on Catholics), then the justices could rest easy that the corrupt priest could signify official morality gone awry. But if the concern was over an honest discussion of racism, who would signify the racist? It was asking too much to allow for a semiotic regime in which all white people could signify as racists, and all Black people as the objects of racism. Thus, a new line had to be drawn between the signification of the racist and the use of racial epithets. Indeed, consonant with my argument that the problem films comprised a popular medium for training white America to a new sensibility toward social issues, I think it quite possible that the distinction that emerged in an effort to differentiate prejudicial speech from epithet underwrites, rather than merely foreshadows, what we today understand as hate speech. I want, therefore, to read more closely and diligently around the brief text that strikes down the censoring of *Pinky*, as well as its intertexts.

"Prejudice" and Epithet

Birth of a Nation and *Pinky* were both banned as "prejudicial"; they were thought capable of inciting racial violence that a municipality might not be able to contain. This catch phrase, used by censorship boards set up after the *Mutual* decision, was something different than a list of images to be censored that had been negotiated by the industry in their film codes. But both were clearly informed by the psychology of film reception that had been articulated by the Hays Code.

From 1915 until early 1952, when *Pinky*'s censoring was upheld by the Texas court of appeals (before later being overturned in the Supreme Court case), censorship based on prejudiciality had meant, in practice, that films should not contain segments that might produce race riots, especially segments that might incite revolt by Blacks. In this older connotative regime, "prejudice" was more a legal than a psychological concept, and the censorship of specific images rested on a belief that such images would have a direct, mass effect. By contrast, the concept of prejudice in the problem film, influenced by liberal social science and the emerging rhetoric of the civil rights movement, suggested that individual psychopathology, like a contagious disease, caused interpersonal harm that had only an indirect, cumulative, national effect. Thus, the sum of all the particular instances of discrimination was a blight on America's moral standing in the community of nations. Indeed, echoing the idea used to justify American involvement in World War II—that the eyes of the world were looking—the diegetic discourse of prejudice in *Pinky* includes the judge (upon hearing the dispute over Pinky's inheritance) pronouncing that: "The eyes of the world are on this little town."

Although *Pinky* contained this new discourse about prejudice, Kazan had difficulty signifying the racism to which it referred. The "unprejudiced" white character's self-reflexive discourse about prejudice suggested that initiating a personal search banished prejudice instead of obscuring its presence to its possessor. The white doctor/boyfriend (Tom) informed Pinky that he had "look[ed] inside" himself to see whether he harbored prejudice.[9] "I'm a doctor, a scientist," he pleaded, "I hope I don't have anything like that." On the cusp of the civil rights movement, the white Southerner's anxiety about elusive and illegible African heritage was mirrored by the Northerner's fears that an undetected prejudice would reveal a truth about the self. The film did not recognize the racism in Tom's willingness to not see Pinky as Black; instead, it was Pinky's assertion of a racial identity that was not so easy to see that breached their relationship. Thus, the internal discourse about prejudice operated as a relay between Pinky's attempts to produce her self as Black and Tom's refusal to read her as other than white.

By contrast, the emergent issue, the "real" problem of "bigotry," is narratively produced in a scene in which two drunken white men whistle and yell lewd remarks at a woman they presume to be white. Subtly, the very presence of a woman alone on a country road at dusk justifies their growing ardor. Only when they shine their light on their prey do they perceive her race as Black. Anticipating the contemporary legal concepts of sexual harassment and hate crime, they shift from sexualized banter to violence as they attempt to rape her, and she narrowly escapes. The logic of the scene is not that discovery of her "true race" eliminates their final inhibitions about taking liberties with a single woman. Instead, their escalation is a product of their rage at being fooled, at their discovery of the passing that she cannot help but live. Here the film tries to proceed through a logic that separates sex and violence, one not unlike that adopted by feminists a few decades later; what begins as drunken lust is transformed into an act of sheer racist-sexist violence. The attempt to perform this split is already complicated by the understanding of rape that is present in the film code, if not, as feminists would indeed point out, in society generally. The code dealt with rape as a subcategory of sex, not of violence. The problem with images of rape was that they might ignite desires in ordinary men, not that they provided a "school for criminals." Thus, the mechanism of the image of attempted rape in *Pinky* is extraordinarily complex: the plausibility of the scene rests on, and to some extent critiques, particular ideas of race and masculinity.

But the "real" issue, we would judge today, is the erasure of a critical axis of gender/race relations; that is, Black women's double history of subjection to white men. On one hand, they have been forced to be (privately) available to white men as women; on the other, they have been the (sexualized) object of public racial violence. In the first case, Black women's situation has been represented at remove through representations and narration of the "mixed" child whose public presence proves but elides her private absence. Whether explicitly rape or, as poignantly narrated in texts like Harriet Jacobs's *Incidents in the Life of a Slave Girl* (1861), via a calculus of extreme disadvantage, the abuse of the Black woman's body and psyche by white men becomes the means of damaging something perceived to be the property of a Black man and a demonstration of the Black man's powerlessness to protect what is his.

In the second case, the sexual dimension of racist violence is publicly obscured because, after a certain point in time (perhaps),[10] it was more palatable to white audiences to stand "witness" to the horror of lynching (usually represented as a violence enacted exclusively on Black men) than it was to "witness" white men's rape of Black women. To see the attempted rape as only sex or only violence ignores the deep logic of racism in which the Black woman has no right to her body—as a woman, as Black, or as a desiring person. The legal history of adjudicating racist violence, still deeply unresolved by the time *Pinky* was released, forces two different concepts of due process to collide. Precedence, at the time, was given to the possibility of violence resulting from racial co-presence, a due process issue for a municipality that would be forced to cope with the results. Due process in the sense that we popularly conceive it today was thus only secondarily applied to the individual victim of white rage expressed as the lynch mob (which was, shockingly, just losing its official sanction at the time of *Pinky*'s production).[11] For the mixed-race body, whose heritage is precisely a confounding of the violation of Black bodies or the refusal of their desires, the double violation of due process is, as I will theorize further in chapter 4, a wrong with no hope of legal compensation.

The slurs that help shift the tone in this crucial scene and mark Pinky's attackers as racists (rather than mere rapists) soon became an intolerable means of signifying racism. A newly, if only partially, morally concerned Hollywood now began a new regime of anxiety about film content: it scrutinized its product not for unleashing interracial hatred or lust, but for using racial epithets (de Grazia and Newman 1982, 67). At the same moment as some interracial relationships were making it to the screen, the film industry began to discourage the use of racial slurs. One iconic sign, the cross-racially desired or desiring Black body, was now permitted, though rarely used; meanwhile a powerful linguistic sign, the white constantive utterance of bigotry, was prohibited. These were countervailing, not complementary changes. When they had been part of racist humor in film, slurs had not been viewed as "fighting words" but as part of the entertainment, and thus they had not been subject to the original "prejudiciality" charge. But in the late 1940s and early 1950s, "slurs," even those intended to signify the racism of the speaker, were viewed as universally impeding the progress of the Black citizenry. This concern about racist dialogue, the growing popular interest in narratives about the plight of twentieth-century "Negros," and the subsequent striking down of other race-related censorship provisions are often viewed by film historians as the crucial breaks that enabled a new kind of Black participation in film and a new willingness to discuss America's race problem through film. Ominously though, once white characters could no longer verbally indicate their racism, the Black body had to signify the racism to which it was subject, a kind of mirror icon, the body-object of the slur left unperformed. Thus, the policing of dialogue helped insure that the Black body was simultaneously index and icon—evidence of the problem and the problem itself.

But *Pinky* never quite replaced the logic of prejudiciality with its new discourse of prejudice. The content of the film's ending reinstated both the legal logic of *Mutual* and the moral logic of the Code's human law/natural law division. When Pinky secured her inheritance in court, the judge reluctantly accepts the "law of man" over the more primordial if ambiguous "interests" that intended to forever divide Black from white communities. Even though Pinky dissipated her personal ownership of the property by turning the mansion into a training facility for Black nurses and clinic for Black children, her noble project did not offset her violation of white space—the plantation and the white man's body. As if addressing the Supreme Court's growing scorn for the rubric of prejudiciality, the fictional character of the judge in *Pinky* concluded the property trial with this admonition: "Pinky, you have won your case, but I doubt whether justice has been served for your people or the people of this town."

In *Quality* (Ricketts Sumner 1946), the novel on which *Pinky* was based, the racist townspeople—that is, racists of a certain kind—burn the plantation, a violence that the film seems unwilling or unable to contain as its moral. The film, in contrast, chooses an uplifting ending in a form that aligns it much more with the women's films of the 1940s than with the cinema verité (for example, Flaherty's *Louisiana Story,* 1948) that showed life as it was in the period. As an image, the burning plantation was too much like the racial slurs that pseudo-liberal Hollywood had become anxious to suppress. Nonetheless, the film averts its eyes from the white body that commits racist violence and ends with a close-up of Pinky, gazing Joan of Arc–like, toward the horizon.

The Dominoes Fall

The series of cases following from the *Burstyn* decision (ending censorship of *The Miracle*) are part of a careful gambit of legal precedent building and disassembling aimed at ending film censorship through a reconsideration of the meaning of film content and form. Most film historians have considered the fifteen or so state and federal cases of the late 1940s and early 1950s to have effectively ended broad censorship, even while the judgments made room for the category of obscenity as the sole remaining self-evident type of images that would not be permissible in movies. Those who write histories of this period give two reasons for this breakdown of film censorship: first, the increased concern about anti-Semitism in the wake of the Nazi regime; and second, the sweeping social changes occurring during and in the immediate postwar years.

Several mid-1940s films about anti-Semitism that might have been censored as "prejudicial," "violent," or "sacrilegious" were released, uncensored, after extensive script review. Yet, three of the "color bar" films were censored only two years later. Perhaps, as Donald Bogle (1989) and Gerald Mast (1982) have both suggested, the rising support for Black civil rights and the massive demographic shifts during the war and postwar period—which first saw employment and urbanization of Southern Blacks and working-class women and then desertion of Black men in urban ghettos and the banishment of white (and to a lesser extent, Black) women to suburbs—had an impact on the kinds of issues Americans wished both to discuss and contest the representation of in film. Indeed, issues of migration and Southern versus Northern racism are significant narrative elements in the films about race of this period. As a result, there were often different poster and ad campaigns directed at the Southern versus Northern and Western audiences, and distribution figures from the period suggest that the South represented less than one eighth of the viewing market. But these commonsense accounts, though suggesting the social context of the censorings, do not take into account the interrelationship between types of film censorship, especially the implicit inscription of racial censorship as sexual censorship. Nor do they grapple with the evolving aesthetic form of film itself.

It was much more than a regrettable Puritanism that allowed the courts to maintain the "sex"-related areas of the censorship while striking down the "race"-related ones. When combined in particular ways, existing tropes that linked race and sexuality made it possible to interpret films as "about" race but not "about" sexuality. The elevation of the passing Pinky to a sort of Joan of Arc in a racist world is accomplished explicitly through her de-sexualization. The broad hermeneutic that deflected the issue of sexuality onto the issue of race in part offered the courts the opening to consider them separately. Thus, race and heterosexuality become even more inextricably bound. In order to show racial censorship to be unenlightened but not licentious, and in order to argue that censorship suppressed a legitimate critique of racism rather than promoting "social equality," the courts needed another category of images and another set of legal language with which to compare the censorship provisions and the films that they enjoined. "Obscenity" was increasingly enlisted as this commonsense category of the banishable—but constantly invoked—category of images.

The interdependence of censorship areas is clearest when the self-evidence of obscenity is invoked to show up the vagueness of virtually every other criterion for censoring film. It is always easier to express disdain for an absent offense than it is to decide how nearly an object under scrutiny fits into an actionable category. The crucial *Burstyn* case itself establishes this contingency as a legal logic. According to the written judgment:

> Since the term "sacrilegious" is the sole standard under attack here, it is not necessary for us to decide, for example, whether a state may censor motion pictures under a clearly drawn statute designed and applied to prevent the showing of obscene films. That is a very different question from the one now before us. (505–6)

Instead of contemplating the similarities between, say, the kisses or attempted rape scene in *Pinky* and scenes in other films thought to be self-evidently obscene, the courts could shift their attention to the lack of warrant in these specific cases of censorship based on restrictions concerning race and religion versus the presumed consensus against obscenity in the abstract.

While subsequent cases seem to chip away at the areas for concern articulated in the censorship statutes, the end of film censorship was not as simple as declaring one provision after another

Figure 7. *Roberto Rossellini's film* The Miracle *(1948) offended Catholics and the courts with its risqué blend of sex and religion. Actress Anna Magnani portrayed a peasant woman who believes she has encountered St. Joseph and thereafter finds herself pregnant and the object of scandal.*

vague and unconstitutional. Rather, minute shifts in the forms of signs—from icons to symbols, from indexes to icons—meant that raced and sexed bodies were no longer representations of sexual perversion or members of a race, but potentially signifiers of the larger sexual and racial problematics. Only iconic representations of sex would remain as the censorable "obscene," but even these representations would be hard to define. Evidently, one man's critique is another man's turn-on, and municipalities increasingly coped with bawdy movies by restricting where they could be shown; thus, pornography because less like a movie and more like an extension of sex trade activities.[12]

Sacrilege and Race versus Sexuality

Significantly, the morality tales of both *Pinky* and *The Miracle* hinge on stories of sexuality and misrecognition. In *Pinky*, the white doctor/boyfriend misrecognizes his love object as white, while in *The Miracle*, a mentally disabled shepherdess mistakes a passing stranger for St. Joseph and bears his child out of wedlock under the scornful eyes of townspeople and priests. But the films were censored for their respective "prejudicial" *(Pinky)* and "sacrilegious" aspects *(The Miracle)*. Though it was the linkage with sex that made the "prejudice" and "sacrilege" evident, neither the censors nor the courts directly addressed sexuality. Indeed, the Court had to dislink the offending thematic from the narrative vehicle in order to strike down as vague many of the provisions detailed in film codes, while stating confidently that it would not extend its efforts to end censorship provisions covering "obscene" films. Obscenity kept being reconstituted as the gnomon[13] space, the issue that didn't need to be dealt with "here." But by remaining phantasmal, obscenity and the presumed consensus on banning it were stabilized. Indeed, in a series of subsequent cases over the next five years, sexuality-related representations like prostitution, abortion, and rape that had been either banned or that required "depiction" with "good taste" were taken out of the censors' reach. Formerly taboo subjects, ranging from interracial relations to premarital sex and homosexuality, became the overt focus of the emerging genre of problem films.

The value of the moving image had changed; the "Negro problem" films criticized racism through use of plots or representations that directly contravened the implicitly segregationist sensibility of *Mutual* and explicitly racially anxious provisions of the Hays Code. But it is crucial to note that the image was no longer an icon with the power to cause rioting or imitation.

Legally, films were only moving, fictional versions of the other organs of the free press, and only incidentally images. The signs that required suppression were no longer images but words—the slurs and taunts that had once been incidental elements in white entertainment.

4.

ACTING UP
The Performing American

Signs of Apartheid

I am making a lot out of *Pinky,* so I should confess to my selection process. I found *Pinky* by accident. An elderly colleague, a historian of film stereotyping who knew I was interested in Madonna's *Like a Prayer* video (1989), axed by Pepsi because of its interracial kiss, mentioned to me that a previously censored and then nearly unavailable film was being shown that night on American Movie Classics. I was at the height of my Madonna madness and imagined her as the progenitor of every subversive image. I didn't remember to watch the film but instead happened to flip by that channel en route to my usual dinnertime dose of *Miami Vice* reruns. I missed the beginning of the film and only half watched the rest. I found the acting uneven at best, the melodramatic plot clichéd, and the representations of African Americans to be deeply stereotypical and often painful to watch. Why, I wondered, did anyone bother to censor the film? A cursory foray into the reviews of the time revealed that concerns about acting shot through every aspect of the film's reception and censorship; implicit in the reviews was anxiety about, or outrage at, the possibility of passing and of acting the part of a passing character. The casting choice of Jeanne Crain (a white musicals actress with little dramatic experience) in

Figure 8. *Jeanne Crain seeks solid acting ground in* Pinky.

the role of the passing Black woman (chosen over Lena Horne!) raised questions for me about how the issue of acting related to plausibility, to realness, and to the possibility of conveying authentic experience (of Blackness to white audiences, but also of Black reality to Black audiences). The subsequent references to the film in histories of censorship or of African Americans on screen also collapsed the problem of acting race, as worked through in the film's time period, with later beliefs about the ethics of passing.[1] Gary Null's description of the film in his much-cited *Black Hollywood: The Negro in Motion Pictures* (1975) is typical:

> In 20th Fox's *Pinky*, a nurse returns to her home in the South after posing as white in Boston. After a number of episodes that show Pinky going through conflicts about her masquerade, she finally gives up her false white identity along with her white boyfriend and opens up a nursing home for black children. (125)

Null's description is very much a product of the 1960s Black Power era that criticized interracial relations and valorized not just Africanicity but, as Gates (1987) puts it, the *blackness* of blackness as well. Null understands Pinky as *posing* rather than *passing;* as being disturbed by a masquerade, rather than profoundly conflicted by her attachment to two worlds where she has legitimate claim; as having an individual, "false white identity," which rose and fell with her "white boyfriend," rather than a "true" or positive hybrid identity that she shared with a class of mixed-race persons. Instead of placing the passing Black woman within the postwar discourse of labile racial identity, Null and his contemporaries measure her against a 1970s conception of *essential* Black identity.

But this lack of sensitivity to the film's historical position did not surprise me as much as the disjuncture in its assessment by the popular critics of its day. For example, the *New Yorker*'s reviewer believed that

> . . . the acting is excellent. Jeanne Crain is quite persuasive as the heroine and Ethel Barrymore and Ethel Waters lend their usual authority to the respective roles of the gruff but kindly Southern aristocrat (the dowager) and an understanding and incredibly patient old washer woman, who is the heroine's grandmother. (McCarten 1949)

Notice that acting the racially liminal character requires artistic persuasion, a kind of ongoing argument, as if the plausibility of acting-passing is always in question. In contrast, the racial stock pieces merely relay an "authority" that has already linked their race with a character and in which, to some extent, their race is *equivalent to* their character. These characters are already legible racial signs.

Taking the opposite evaluative pole, but boiling *Pinky*'s plot-line down to the level of absurdity as an even-more scoffing challenge to the possibility of passing, the *New Republic*'s reviewer argued that the film failed, and that:

> As far as the race "angle," pure-white Negro girls don't go North from a cabin, become trained nurses, and then return home to defeat single-handed the rampant hatred of a poor-white-trash community. (Hatch 1949, 173)

Oblivious to the actuality of passing women's success in transgressing white space, ignoring the wild popularity of the story in women's pulp fiction, Hatch here evades the question of race and acting by deeming the part itself, and the job it does in the plot, to be an impossible space. He also relies on the same trope as *Gentleman's Agreement* to situate racism in "poor white trash," despite the fact that the racism exhibited in *Pinky* is primarily that of fallen white aristocrats and the legal and judicial system they expect to support them. These extreme views about *Pinky*'s acting directed me to rethink the popular notion that "serious" acting in film entails an authenticity of characterization, a kind of universalizing move to represent what is "true" in "all of us." (Where people seem to disagree is only over whether any actors can—if sufficiently talented and having done the proper research- act any part.) It occurred to me that *Pinky* might have landed in the middle of a crisis concerning the status and role of acting. At a minimum, the acting in the film was part of a struggle, in drama, over the appropriate form of representation. Given that the film is itself about acting race, *Pinky* also seems to have been implicated in the post–World War II crisis about signifying race in the popular media, which was used predominantly, though by no means exclusively, by white audiences. This crisis was only partially diffused when the Supreme Court struck down censorship prohibitions that were concerned with racial conflict and racial representation. But was it true that acting always entailed attention to "realness"? Weren't limits placed on who was allowed to represent whom, and on which classes of people lacked the capacity to universalize emotion? Weren't some people hence condemned only to represent the (supposed) particularity of their experience?

Acting History/The Historicity of Acting

Early film acting congealed from a variety of class forms, regionally and racially marked: mime, burlesque, revues (especially minstrel), and a kind of naturalism that emerged with early travelogue and quasi-documentary film. As Roberta Pearson (1992) has shown in her work on the Biograph Company's development of a trademark acting style, silent film acting developed into a stock of extreme and static gestures that signaled emotion and carried the plot forward. Emerging during Jim Crow and operating under a film censorship ethos influenced by the legal rationale of *Plessy v. Ferguson* (which viewed racial violence as a near-certain outcome of racial mixing), film production and consumption was largely segregated, temporally and spatially. Theaters commonly had late night shows for Black patrons or required Blacks to sit in the balcony. Laws in some states and municipalities forbade Blacks and whites from acting together on the same stage. Movies followed suit well into the teens, using blackfaced white actors to play "negro" roles. However, with a few notable exceptions, like the actors in *The Birth of a Nation*, these blackfaced actors did not so much represent Black people as behave as formal devices to signal plot turns or to mirror the interiority of the white[2] actors who were the plot's primary (but mute) agents. Even after their admission to Hollywood film, actors of color rarely acted on their own behalf.

Given these considerations, it will be useful to detail the effect the "talkies" (films with integrated sound) had on raced acting. But this, in turn, requires a brief review of the Peircean[3] semiotic scheme[4] that has been so usefully extended by film theorists like de Lauretis (1984) and Eco (1984) and complexly reread by Deleuze (1986). Peirce describes signs as having gradations of relation to their referents. I want to discuss only those called icon and index and to consider what these might mean for raced acting. An icon is a sign that has a visual relation to its referent, and in this sense, I want to suggest, it operates much like a noun. The drift away from strict iconicity might be accomplished through substitutions on the model of metaphor. Though we know semiotic constructs are not necessary, iconic signs present themselves as only one step removed from essence and, therefore, demand to be treated as *things*. For Peirce, indexical signs have a logical relation to, but do not exactly mirror, their referent. In the classic example, smoke is an indexical sign for fire. By extension, I want to suggest, indexical signs operate more like verbs in that they are a present-absence whose meaning is secured by the interpreter's knowledge of a prior set of interrelations. Thus, smoke is interpreted as "burning," which then points to its source, fire. An index necessarily carries with it a universe of meaning and demands to be treated not as a thing but as a story. We can understand an indexical when we partake in the universe of connections on which the index relies. Symbols are considered the most abstract, a sort of vehicle between a remembered materiality and a cultural abstraction. Symbols are the most evidently arbitrary signs but, at the same time, they are the bearers of strong cultural associations. In this sense, they demand to be read as messengers of considerable import, capable of mediating the obvious and the divine and easing the metaphysical slide between them. It is the sublation of its arbitrariness that makes the index of interest to me as I sort through the possibilities of race and acting.

In her own revisions of Peircean semiotics, de Laurelis (1984) has pointed out, in relation to the image of a woman, that orders of sign—iconicity, indexicality, symbolicity—may be simultaneously present by degrees. Of course, the same holds true for other complex cultural significations, in this case race. But I want to further suggest that the legibility (the "ground" as Peirce puts it when describing the reception of signs) of orders of sign may change. For example, blackfaced acting of the teens seems to have operated largely indexically, constituting both a literal present-absence of the Black body (even Black actors initially acted in blackface), and a figurative present-absence in that blackfaced acting in film operated as a displaced performance of the emotions of white characters whose actors could not avail themselves of dialogue in order to explain their motives or intentions. In this way, the blackfaced and, later, *Black* actor is a kind of caption box indexing the interiority of the white actor's character.[5] This difference in the work of blackfaced acting and, complexly, by association, the evocation of Black personality, is critical to our understanding of why the social crisis over "the Negro problem" might have found its cultural articulation in the white female form of melodrama—indeed, in the body of a white woman who was, impossibly enough, acting white in (invisible) blackface.

While actors in and out of blackface used the highly gestural acting form of early cinema, Black raced bodies signaled a different interpretive scheme. White supremacism inflicted a terrible wrong on the bodies that were indicated and used in this way, and we commonly think of this as racist stereotyping of characters. But in addition, the reality of Black lives and Black creative labor disappeared when Black raced bodies were recruited to do the work of narrative (by indexing plot turns) or of characterization for others (by somatizing the interiority of the "white" characters around whom the plot revolved). The latter, in part, explains the surface frenzy of the acting style that this use of signs enabled. For example, the entry of "the Mexican" meant a fight would ensue; the imminent surprise or misrecognition that actors (acting as white characters) were supposed to be "experiencing," but which fell outside their gestural repertoire, was relayed to the viewer through a specific range of hyper gestures: the wide-eyed, open-mouthed incredulity of blackfaced bodies. Like the classic Peircean indexical, these racially and ethnically constructed indexicals did not require the audience to correlate an image with a referent person, but rather relied on the white audience's pre-established association[6] of the Black raced body with a set of perceived or repressed causal relations and, albeit racist, ideas about the violence or primitive emotionality of Latino or Black persons.[7]

Racial marks in this period of screen acting, although their iconic reference to actual Black persons was clearly simultaneously present, did not primarily signify Black presence (or, conversely, force an honest contemplation of Black absence). Rather, they indexed a logically *prior* set of presuppositions about the Black body. Raced signs operated like verbs waiting to connect actor and emotion-object. They were not a presence because they did not take up "space" in the diegesis. They were not in diegetic time; rather, they became a *condition of possibility* for diegetic time. Far from simply trading in ugly stereotypes, understood as a static interpretive practice of reading image onto "real people," these signs deployed and sublated a whole history of racial hostility. The white audience did not, I think, evaluate these representations in terms of realism, because the blackfaced body signified as a relation, not as a representation. Similarly, at least in scenes of gender misrecognition, male-male desire operated as a transitive verb forever deprived of an object; such fleeting indexes did not refer to *a* homosexual, but rather delayed the presumption of heterosexuality while activated.[8] This is not to say that such in-dexes were not homophobic or racist. Rather, they invoked racist and homophobic regimes of meaning in different ways than the concept of stereotyping suggests; they relied on racist and homo-phobic ideas at one step removed. Our retrospective reading of these films is that any sign of blackness was intended to refer, and was interpreted as referring, to an actual person, i.e., that the signs were "representations." This led to a conviction—shared by Ethel Waters, as I will later show—that prejudice could be overcome by more profoundly and authentically acting (or really, being) Black. The power of authentic presence was understood to be capable of decentering inauthentic and inauthentically held prejudice. This was a basic premise of the civil rights movement and, I suggest, of all of the identity-based new social movements that followed. But the prominence of "visibility" politics was not just an imitation of the Black efforts, nor even a tactical adoption of Black strategies, but rather coextensive with an entire shift in semiogenesis in the mid- to late twentieth century. This understanding of the highly stereotyped and undeniably racist Black characterizations of clas-sic film until the late 1940s produced the hope among 1950s to 1970s filmmakers that replacing negative stereotypes with more "authentic" Black characters might strike a blow against prejudice. But the enduring damage inflicted by the blackfaced mime was not so much that whites largely believed that this was how "real" Black people actually were, but that in expropriating the raced body as a verb, the personness, agency, and play of the Black body were disavowed. The subtle apartheid built into the very opera-tion of these signs made the raced body operate in and as a sign of a separate regime of meaning that persists (though in differ-ent forms) today. It almost always "means something" to have a Black buddy, Black bad guy, or interracial couple in a film or on TV, even if it only now means "we are not using the Black body to mean anything particular." Critics in part redouble this surplus meaning of the Black body when, for example, Black sci-fi charac-ters are scrutinized to understand how they make meaning differ-ently than white characters might have. But this critical attention also multiplies the possible meanings of Black bodies, potentially rendering the Black body so polysemous that it loses its ability to indict the bigotry that outlives blackfaced bodies' semiotic role.

In the late 1940s, the Black body as such made a fleeting appearance in film as a representation of Black actuality, and the dozen Black actors who brilliantly played the objects of racism nearly had America by the heart. But in *Pinky*, the use of indexes of whiteness and Blackness and the way the film constitutes time through space banishes white viewers' recognition of the racist present into the past. Although there are indications in the film-text that the events occur quite specifically in the viewer's present (i.e., the immediate post–World War II period), the narrative device of sending Pinky from the "time" of the North to the "rhythm" of the South leaves the viewer (and certainly the contemporary viewer, who is likely to miss the little cues as to the film's time) uncertain about the universality of American racism or historical

Figure 9. *Early white cinema, such as* The Love Mart *(1927), displaced white emotion onto Black bodies, evacuating Black experience from the screen. Still from D. J. Leab,* From Sambo to Superspade *(Boston: Houghton Mifflin, 1975).*

particularity of the Black experience so lushly undergoing representation. *Pinky* was not so much about what the raced person is like "now" as it was about what the transhistorical Black experience had been in relation to white systems of power—challenging or sublating the national popular memory of what Black-white relations have been. Cinematically, *Pinky* is on the cusp of a period of Black representation that is "about" racism and only about Black experience insofar as being-an-object-of-prejudice can be produced as universal.[9]

Sound, Class, and Narrative

The semiotic loading of gesture and look may be clearer if we compare the use of racialized hypergestures with a similar invocation, in silent film, of expressions of male-male desire, which reestablished a heterosexuality that could not itself be expressed. Usually framed as moments of sex/gender misrecognition or, in some rare cases, as a lingering gaze, these queer moments did *not*—as those who trace the tentacles of "gay identity" into the past have suggested— "represent" *homosexuals*. Rather, they indexed heterosexuality since, in such a moment, otherwise-invisible heterosexuality got noticed because it had been momentarily deferred. But while the blackfaced white actor's makeup continually signed an acted blackness, even the most iconically homosexual character was only queer *in motion*. Unlike the blackfaced white actor, whose racial marking was static and referred interpretation of his gestures to a second register, signifying the deferral of heterosexual desire required, well, acting *queer*. These older styles of acting relied heavily on "stereotypes"—of objects, dress codes, locations, etc.—but in differing degrees. In particular, sets tied the gesture of the blackfaced actor to cultural ideas of Black people (the watermelon coupled with the wide grin), while camp gestures were detached from the body of the actor who performed them (masculine dress or masculine setting contradicted by the limp wrist that seemed ready to fall off). But these signs of blackness and queerness utilized associations (none the less racist and homophobic for being mobile) to constitute character, move plot, or indicate mood. Bereft of dialogue, silent films used anything and everything in a variety of ways to sign character, plot, and moods. The shift from silent film to talkies would be crucial to the performance of race because the new technology altered the relationship between acting and dialogue.

By the teens, film producers sought to legitimate cinema by appealing to the perceived aesthetic preferences and architectural demands of middle-class entertainment seekers, a potential market that seemed curious about cinema but appreciated neither the low-brow "nickel" movie nor the seedy, noisy, ethnic space of the "nickelodeon" where it was shown. By the late teens, the outrageously expensive $2 feature-length film based on a historical theme or reproducing a classic play was emerging as the ideal form of movie, even if it took another decade for it to capture a significant portion of the market. The greater emphasis on narrative, the increased need to relate action and emotion, and the interest in extending the range of film's cultural capital by producing opera encouraged those who were rapidly developing a range of film-sound technologies. The introduction of sound, and especially synchronized sound, secured the place of these longer, middle-class-oriented entertainments and narrowed the new style of film acting as film companies began to recruit actors from the "legitimate stage." Not only did the new wave of stage-trained actors already know how to deliver dialogue, but they also arrived with a history on the stage—however minimal or lackluster—that was believed to improve the status of films in which they appeared, thereby increasing the cultural capital of the industry.

Critical reception of the very idea of talking films was mixed; the sound quality was deemed "unrealistic" and synchronized dialogue introduced a second level of possibly offensive and censorable items. Antimovie activists who questioned the moral value of the new medium had grown alarmed about Hollywood sex scandals; they had long argued that film's visual dimension encouraged viewers to confuse stars with the characters they played. Immersed in a psychic "dream world" of movies, fans might emulate the offscreen behavior of their idols. But for movie advocates, sound solved the problem of the audience's potential for adoring unworthy stars: the new influx of "real" actors would replace the intangible "it" quality of silent films stars with a truly enviable quality called "personality," thus securing movies' value as an uplifting populist entertainment. In 1930 *Commonweal* magazine's Maurice L. Ahern offered this description of a late 1920s Hollywood deluged by "ladies and gentlemen of the legitimate stage" in "Hollywood Horizons":

> The public can no longer be fooled and so droves of heavy lovers and impassioned ladies of the premicrophone days are drifting back to the overalls of the filling station and the apron of the kitchen. . . . Not all the mimes of the other cinema days were brainless beauties with unpleasant voices. There is a goodly group upon whom sound has had the same effect as sun and rain on spring flowers. The glorious Garbo seems even more so as one listens to her throaty, accented speech. Lois Moran's personality has become vividly defined and given a vibrant quality through Movietone. Janet Gaynor's voice fully verifies the winsome personality we had always associated with her. (See Mast 1982, 308)

By complexly reorganizing class, ethnic, and gender values in film, the shift to sound transformed movies into a medium in which the essential *personness* of the actor, inescapably revealed through qualities of the voice, was newly relevant to the character he or she would portray. But notice that in Ahern's formulation the actors are really like the characters they play; however, they *do not* play roles that are like themselves. This slight asymmetry in the identity between actor and character privileges the dream world of the movies. Fans expect a gap between movies and life; they do not want to see the actor's real life as ordinary but rather want reassurance that the actor is not less than his or her screen image. Equally, it was the lack of access to voice that allowed silent acting to so easily "fool" an audience. The technological innovation of synchronized sound, not acting itself, allowed audiences to discover the truth of "personality" in the quality of their idol's voice. Sound revealed something that acting alone could not convey and, indeed, carried with it an implicit criticism of the "it" quality that could mask a lack of "personality." The blossoming of the pleasantly voiced might weed out those who lacked personality, but acting in itself did not reveal the falseness of the silent actor.

Figure 10. *Classic Hollywood's highly stylized acting style, as seen in* Night Flight *(1933), starring Helen Hayes and John Barrymore. Still from J. R. Parish and R. L. Bowers,* The MGM Stock Company *(New York: Bonanza Books, 1972).*

Initially, sound only supplemented older facial and gestural conventions with the dialogue delivery styles of classical theater, comedy, and minstrelsy. Soon, however, dialogue began to take up some of the labor that blackfaced mime and theatricality in general had accomplished. In a short order, film shifted from being a nonlinguistic montage to a visualized novel. Before sound, gestures had punctuated and pointed to the essence in the unacted ("profilmic") that makes the real *real*. But crude early sound technology removed this possibility: actors had to deliver their lines while standing or sitting motionless near cumbersome hidden microphones. Thus deprived of their gestural range and even of "natural" movement, what was said on film was dissociated from the actor's body and became a potentially more credible carrier of plot and characterization. The good voice and the ability to deliver dialogue would soon be privileged over the ability to perform static facial contortions and gestures that had been the hallmarks of silent film acting.

Body and voice were reunited with the introduction of the traveling sound boom, but this innovation presented a new strain on acting. The actor had to be able to walk and deliver lines to the camera, a requirement that created an entirely new phenomenologic of acting. Improvements in camera tracking and panning allowed the actor's body to create a physical continuity between the dialogic and narrative elements within a highly mobile film space. By the end of the 1930s, this highly stylized form of movement and delivery consolidated into what we now recognize as the acting style of Hollywood's classic period. Dialogue and the new acting it required altered racial and queer representation. Black characters were no longer as necessary to the plot, and the phrases that indicated a character's damning overfamiliarity with queer words were easier to rout out.

But by the time *Pinky* was produced a decade later, this Classic style of acting was already being challenged by the Method, well established on the New York stage and introduced into film by directors and actors who had come from the theater.[10] In the Method, actors did not so much re-perform the stock of gestures and into-

Figure 11. *The Method embodied: James Dean.*

Figure 12. *The roots of Method acting run deep and include the performance style of Black independent cinema, as exemplified in* The Scar of Shame *(1927), produced by the Colored Players Film Corporation.*

nations that signed narrative and characterological elements (as in classic film) as they attempted to produce, as if for the first time, the very emotions their character would have had. This resulted in "researching" parts and learning to connect the events that produced the character's proposed emotions with events in the actor's own life that had produced similar emotions. Actors no longer acted a part but, instead, reenacted the primal elements of their own biography; the surface of the actor's body projected emotions, but their source lay in his or her own secret memories.

It would be a mistake to assume, as does the popular description of this acting style, that the actor *became* his or her character. As I showed earlier, classic Hollywood's white actors were also understood as having an intimate similarity to their characters. But in classic Hollywood, extreme stylistics, codified as gestures and a quality of voice, signified the actor's occupation of the characterological space. The classic actor performed—with all the artistic

nuance and personal spin possible—the stock gestures and into-
nations that were considered quintessential to an emotion or to
marking the kind of person they portrayed.[11]

In the Method, the distance between the memory that produced the actor's surface emotion collapsed into the events that
the narrative proposed for the character. The plausibility of this
collapse was in turn determined by the collapse of the viewer's
own private memories into the space of actor-character. Far from
representing emotion, Method actors believed they broke past interpretation to the primal *experience* of emotion. Completion of
this intimate circuit was the new goal of acting. The moment of
its accomplishment was thought of as dyads of "identification"
that all arrived at the same place. Considerable time and effort
were required to ease the actor and viewer into this gambit of emotional collapse. The frenetic, hysterical compositions of classical
film gave way to a new, visually more complex and protracted cinematic style—disorienting camera angles, long facial close-ups,
tight shots of fetish objects associated with the invoked emotions,
less action, slower delivery of dialogue. This cinematic style, naturalized through the 1970s as cine-realism or what is popularly
called "serious drama," came to dominate Hollywood, at once a
popular discourse about producing one's authentic self and a mass
classroom for a new cultural performance of identity. Its chal-
lengers have been few and emerged later, in the 1980s, with the
neo-Brechtian style associated with the New American Gothic of
David Lynch and the anti-acting styles of 1980s action heroes like
Arnold Schwarzenegger and Jean-Claude Van Damme.[12]

When it arose, the Method also provided two new rationales
for the employment of Black actors. First, in order for a white actor
to perform as Black within Method, she or he would have to call up
personal experiences. But the calculus that suggested that all op-
pressions are essentially the same was only just being established.
In addition, the binary structure of racism meant that what the
white actor "knows" about *being racist* would have to be set aside
in order to recover a sense of *being oppressed* that was more particular and around which mass media discourses did not yet exist.
Second, Black actors could now stand as the sign of the discourse

Figure 13. *Black method actors like James Edwards, here in* Home of the Brave *with Lloyd Bridges and Frank Lovejoy, must hold center stage and defend an acting space that white audiences have sometimes collapsed into autobiography. Still from D. Bogle,* Toms, Coons, Mulattoes, Mammies, and Bucks, *4th ed. (New York: Continuum, 2001; originally published by Viking, 1973).*

of the "Negro problem," indexes whose acting would need to be unhysterical in order not to be read as a displacement of white interiority. This new space for Black presence seems to have been read, at least by commentators of the 1940s and '50s, as a "truth" far more profound than news or documentary film. But because the African Americans who played in these films were understood to be acting their experience, they were seen not as actors but as "real people." The irony of film Method was that the better the performance, the less audiences perceived Black actors to be acting.

Associated with the controversial "problem films,"[13] this new screen acting was almost immediately politicized, and this in a context where film documentary and newsreels had only recently convinced America that film could be a powerful conveyor of "propaganda." Part melodrama, part "message," the "problem film" hung uneasily between the legal categories of "propaganda" and "entertainment."[14] Indeed, one of the disavowals of Kazan's political ambitions for *Pinky* was some critics' contention that the film was mere melodrama. Even the positive reviews argued that some scenes careened outside the tightly guarded bounds of credulity, but the *New Republic*'s Robert Hatch (1949) heaped disdain on the film for trying to address a serious American problem in the wrong generic format: "Aside from the Negro question, the story is standard soap romance for women who are bored enough by their husbands to wonder if dedication would have been an improvement on marriage" (173). The entertaining romance plot seemed capable of destroying the political impact of the film (despite the exhaustive use of didactic monologues that could have been ripped from the script of an American war propaganda film!). Even the amazing job done by Ethel Waters seems not to have read through as political to the critics. By pretending to foreground the story of racism, which the indexical raced body had once sublated, the message film *about* race relations secured a new iconicity for the Black body. Apparently performances like Waters's in *Pinky* or James Edwards's in *Home of the Brave* (1949) could not displace the mute facticity, the iconic sign, of the black surface of their actor-bodies. If, in the old style, raced bodies were largely indexical, Black actors might now be seen as "real people," but not as actors.

The apartheid that had inscribed the labor of Black and white bodies as operating in different orders of signs came crashing headlong when Jeanne Crain, acting in invisible blackface, kissed William Lundigan, who was barely acting at all. The status of performing race—and how *well*—was crucial to the film's censoring: both actors were unimpeachably white, and, thus, the offending kisses were merely a performance of a *misrecognized* miscegenation or, at the most, sexual desire despite, but not *because* of, the illegible mark of Pinky's race. In order to be actionable, the censor and the Texas courts had to assume that audiences believed in the diegetic, rather than the pro-filmic, "reality" of what they saw, and they had to blame Pinky for the love that should not cross race lines. *Pinky* was censored for "not being in the best interests" of the people of Marshall, Texas—a charge, I have argued, that was based in the presumption that race mixing and its representation would cause race riots (see chapter 3). But it is important to note that the race mixing feared in *The Birth of a Nation* was the leering look of a blackfaced man; the riotous rage was designed to protect white femininity. In *Pinky* and the versions of the passing story that appeared in women's magazines of the '40s, the fear of miscegenation centers around the possibility that passing Black women will entrap white men. Here the fear is not of Black men's power but rather of the poverty of white men's racial decoding apparatus. I will return in chapter 5 to the complex of anxieties and hopeful cross-identifications that viewers, especially white women, may have brought to *Pinky*. Now I want to focus more intensely on the relation of acting and blackness so evident in the critical reception of *Pinky*.

Narrative Sublation: Recalling-Forgetting History

As I showed in chapter 3, the prohibition of miscegenation was deeply confused with the legal anxiety over prejudiciality. On the simplest level, the prohibition of miscegenation appears to have applied only to the *presence* of willful interracial congress, not to the visibility of its issue, as the persistence of the "tragic mulatto" character attests. In *Pinky,* the protagonist's whiteness, together with her grandmother's blackness and the almost complete absence of reference to the intermediate generation, only made sense if white viewers recalled their shared cultural memory of generations of violent or transgressive incursions by white men on Black women's bodies. The *New Yorker*'s reviewer (McCarten 1949) traced the edges of this blocked space in white cultural memory, but he could not bring himself to actually recall the sexual dimensions of the history of racist terrorism that the film invokes (and that is required in order to make sense of it):

> The Mendelian intricacies of this young lady's background are not explored in the film, and only a blurred explanation is given to account for her return to her Southern birthplace, where we first meet her after she has spent years as a trained nurse up North in Boston, passing as a white girl as untroubled about her background as any of the Lowells.

The presupposition here that white people are not anxious about their "background" deserves comment. The reviewer must have forgotten that this very issue animates a considerable number of Southern novelists' work and was critical to the plot of the popular Broadway show *Showboat* (twice made into film before *Pinky* and once after, then reinterpreted on Broadway by Tommy Tune in 1995). Indeed, *Quality* author Cid Ricketts Sumner wrote another novel, *But the Morning Will Come* (1949), based on this plot. The Lowells may not worry, but Southerners with elite names like Lee and the Boudreaux certainly did.

Commonweal's reviewer also struggled with the regulative sign of genre, excusing *Pinky* (and Jeanne Crain) for its flaws by associating it with a cinematic cohort.

> Producer Darryl F. Zanuck deserves credit for not attempting to cover the entire racial question in *Pinky*. This film along with *Home of the Brave* and *Lost Boundaries* represents an encouraging start along the right lines in condemning anti-Negro prejudice. Perhaps one day we shall see movies that go the whole way in blasting the false notions of white supremacy. But in the meantime let us be thankful for *Pinky* which succeeds in putting over its themes of tolerance and living for others in a dramatic movie that will reach a large audience. (1949, 15)

But when he runs headlong into the sexualized dimensions of racism that the genre question cannot resolve (i.e., that a melodrama about race must in fact *be* about the construction of families—sex and procreation across racial lines), he beats a hasty retreat. The apparent equivalence between the terms "racial question," "anti-Negro prejudice," and "white supremacy" blur the differences between fears of race mixing and dislike of racism. And, in the space between "anti-Negro prejudice" and "the false notions of white supremacy" lies the body of the Black woman. "Tolerance" and "living for others" are the cost of Pinky's encounter with Southern racism, an encounter that desexualizes her in order to put her back in her Black place of origin.

The acquiescence to desexualization that accompanies Pinky's production of her racial identity and that is so obviously an element in the film is never directly mentioned in the mainstream reviews. Critical response to the film revealed a class or regional fault line in white masculinity's self-conception: the reviewers seemed better able to discuss the scene of attempted rape by the film's most unsavory rednecks—the most violent explanation of the "Mendelian intricacies"—than to entertain the possibility that Pinky's mother had made a different decision when faced with a similar choice. The reviewers seem incapable of accepting the plot on its most superficial level, that is, a mutually loving relationship that is unproblematic until the intrusion of blatant racism transforms romance into tragedy. Here the anxiety about miscegenation is actually anxiety about Black women's agency. Instead of reading the film as the self-production and destruction of a transgressive sexual subject, we must read Pinky as having agency only as a *racial* subject. As *Commonweal's* reviewer put it, Pinky becomes the agent of her destiny when she "learns the meaning of integrity . . . learns about true justice and responsibility" (15). White culture denies the significance for Black women of Pinky's possession of her own desiring body. In order to find a place in even the liberal regime of subjectivities—in order to be a *person*—Pinky must give up anything that has had meaning to her. The same critic continues: "*Pinky* is essentially the story of a person who learns the meaning of life and who finally sees that her own happiness is not the important thing." Pinky can be a (Black) person, but only if she accepts that the "meaning of [her] life" must be the sacrifice of her "happiness," doubly figured as life as white and life with a sexuality.

The Question of Acting

One of the issues complicating *Pinky* is the utilization and racial encoding of both Classical and Method acting, most notably in the two Ethels: Ethel Barrymore[15] acts High Hollywood, while Ethel Waters tries to Method act through her otherwise grotesquely stereotypical lines. As the racially problematic characters, Jeanne Crain and William Lundigan virtually non-act: Lundigan struggles to "not know," and Crain's delivery vacillates between hysteria ("Oh, Tom! I'm a *Negro*") and near nondelivery ("Den . . . ver?") as her racial identity careens between exhibition and obliteration. Lundigan operates as the space of unknowing

Figure 14. *Dr. Thomas Adams (William Lundigan) puzzles over his fiancée's racial identity in* Pinky.

(half of his lines consist of variations on "I don't understand . . ."), while Crain constitutes the space of surplus knowledge. Pinky is supposed to know what it's "like" to be Black and to be white, to live recognized and unrecognized by and as both. The film details Pinky's status as the object of Southern white people's recognition of her as Black after having been un-recognized—or rather, recognized as white—by whites in the North. She is acted on more than she acts.

Unlike the two versions of *Imitation of Life*, which show the struggle between the nonpassable mother and her passing daughter (though ultimately as a means of "proving" that the white protagonist is not "racist"—she cannot "see" race), in Kazan's film both of Pinky's parents are absent. Where the *Imitations* are quite explicitly about the different meanings of passing or not passing, *Pinky* is about the legibility of one's race to others, including, most intimately, one's intended spouse. More than is the case with the two *Imitations*, *Pinky* is about the spatial dimensions of racial recognition: race, its legibility and meaning, is tied to geography rather than class mobility.

The critics faltered over the appropriate terms to describe the labor of acting within the film. Hatch (at the *New Republic*) slides through a series of terms:

> The characterizations are what might be expected. Miss Barrymore plays the irascible tyrant with the bleeding heart, a role in which she and her brother Lionel imitate each other by rotation. Miss Waters displays that combination of rude wisdom and doglike devotion which is as much the Jim Crow stereotype as the happy, irresponsible jig dancing coon. (1949, 173)

Only Barrymore is engaged in acting; she plays, while Waters *displays*. Barrymore's role is explicitly de-gendered, even while its racial status can go unmarked: male or female, the "bleeding heart" is most assuredly white. By contrast, Waters's race is doubly connoted, and she is gendered female through this obsessive reference to race: under the sign of Jim Crow she is the companion piece to the more clearly denotatively male figure.

But while the critic makes a pretense of disliking these forms of performance ("stereotypes"), he abuses the opportunity for social commentary and constitutes the racial companion piece to the "bleeding heart" by using a derogatory term that would otherwise have been unacceptable in public speech (and had become unacceptable as film dialogue). Hatch's treatment of Waters's activity clears up any remaining doubts about his underlying attitude toward what he calls "the Negro question." If the actual brother and sister Barrymores are set apart from their work in film because they "play" a "role" and even "imitate each other," Waters is conflated with Dicey Johnson. Although "rude wisdom" and "doglike devotion" are apparently reviled by the writer, they are attributed as much to Waters as they are to the part of Dicey Johnson. It is not clear whether it is the "characterizations" or the Black people who have been forced to live them that are the object of the critic's hatred: his liberal attack screens a deeper ambivalence about Black presence. Because Waters is said to display rather than act, it is apparently the visibility of Black performance, rather than its lack of fidelity to a referent, that the writer finds so annoying.

In his obligatory description of the plot and association of characters with actors, Hatch makes another split that reveals the complex racial politic of his review. Crain's body moves without acting, while Pinky's body is acted on: "Pinky is deluged with the fear and hatred of the South" even while:

> Miss Crain moves stiffly in a part too unreal to be acted. A Negro girl born in the South, she must walk through town like a Westchester debutante, and resent with amazement the slurs she has known from her cradle.

This is not an account of bad acting but a disavowal of the very possibility of acting passing: "She must make a miracle seem real and she cannot do it—no one could." For Hatch, passing is unrepresentable to the white audience; acting passing is left in the lurch between two concepts of an actor's being-in-the-film. With the Barrymores' bodily distance from role as the sign of whiteness, and Waters's physical conflation with her character as the sign of blackness, Jeanne Crain as Pinky may walk uneasily between them, but she can neither act (be white) nor be a direct presence (be Black) in the film. In formal terms, the reviewer is here refusing the knowledge that the mixed-race body indexes while at the same time refusing to accept Jeanne Crain and the character she plays as an iconic sign of blackness within the film. Clearly, for nearly a century, white viewers and reviewers had been accustomed to seeing white actors taking up the character of a Black person. This criticism of Crain is a major public rejection of a white actor's appearance in blackface, albeit a blackface that relies on audience collusion rather than paint.

Commonweal's reviewer lauds the picture, the director, and the screenplay and, expressing a minority opinion, considers "Jeanne Crain's performance in the title role deeply stirring" (1949, 15). In his other comment on acting he not only fails to mention the Ethels who occupy so much time on screen, but he singles out William Lundigan's performance in the sparse role of Pinky's boyfriend. The critic's curious accolade rings louder as a sympathy vote for the poor actor cast in this role than it does as a real description of an acting job that contributes so little to the story.

[Kazan] has given the movie more than a plot about a Negress who releases her white fiance (William Lundigan handles his difficult role well) and who suffers the indignities of a persecuted minority. (15)

The "release" of the unknowing white boyfriend is, of course, the moral of the passing tale; the mass market magazine versions of the story used similar wording.[16] But in the film version of this complex story of a race-blind love in a racist world, Lundigan's epistemological stance is more important than his role as star-crossed lover whose lack of prejudice ("I'm a doctor, a scientist," he pleaded, "I hope I don't have anything like that") drives him to lock onto a love from which he must be released. Lundigan provides an escape route for white viewers who can neither accept their own racism nor endorse cross-race love. "Dr. Clueless," as I describe the role when I teach this film, is the racial parallel of what Eve Kosofsky Sedgwick describes in terms of heterosexuality in her "Privilege of Unknowing" (1993). Initially, he does not know Pinky is Black and he is still confused when he follows her to her Southern home. He doesn't know "what kind of people live in places like this" and he doesn't understand the significance of Pinky's inheritance of Miss Em's plantation. (He secures the film's general unwillingness to say that Pinky is a relative of Miss Em's—a point made clear in the novel.) He understands something about Southern racism, but his version of antiracism is to continue Pinky's passing in Denver. Lundigan's Tom is the one character who cannot recognize Pinky as Black, but this is no cause for celebrating the brilliance of his acting. It would be closer to the truth to say that Lundigan simply refuses to act. He seems perpetually surprised to find himself on the massive Twentieth Century-Fox lot. He seems surprised that everyone is pretending Jeanne Crain is Black. Most of his mumbled lines seem to be taken from a different script than anyone else is reading. The diegetic solution is identical to Lundigan's apparent choices as an actor. Trying desperately to end the film, Lundigan, as Tom, offers Pinky an obliterating future: "There'll be no more Pinky Johnson." Also trapped between Classical high style and Method, Lundigan seems simply to refuse to enter his role. It seems that he has not "researched" the part, but his near lack of gesture and intonation suggests that he cannot even come up with appropriate gestures of misrecognition—a sign that a raced body might have deployed for him in an earlier regime of acting. To the end, Lundigan refuses to acknowledge Crain's acting race—at any rate, not a very difficult job, but a performance that offers viewers a means of disavowing the politics of the film.

The end of race-based censorship and the displacement of censored signs into the subjectivities of the bodies that were at issue in the problem films created a new popular venue within which to struggle over America's racist past and present. The shift in acting forms and the iconization of the Black body challenged interpretations of race, but deep ambivalence about racial presence remained for both white and Black Americans. The ultimate casualty of that battle is plainly outlined in *Pinky*: the battle of styles and the emerging association of Method with "message" films meant that the characterizations in *Pinky* subtly constitute Black experience as accessible to the white viewer via a system of cathection. The tug between the melodramatic plot, with its Classical style, and cine-realism, with its evocation of the larger social crisis, make interpretation of the film's "message" contingent on perceptions of genre. Though critics hailed problem films as a break into social conscience on the part of Hollywood, the emergence and acceptance of films like *Pinky* may finally have been less a confrontation *with* than a containment *of* the "race problem." In the next chapter, I want to find the edge that hints at the gap between Black expression and white understanding, an edge that can help us see the ethical fragility of the "connection" (or, as I've called it earlier, the cross-race "identification") supposed to take place in white understanding.

5.

TWO CONVERSATIONS
Black and White Americans on Film

Reading (in) "White Time":
Black Performance and the Demand for Literacy

I have the soundest of reasons for being proud of my people.
We Negroes have always had such a tough time that our very
survival in this white world with the dice always loaded against
us is the greatest possible testimonial to our strength, our cour-
age, and our immunity to adversity.

We are close to this earth and to God. Shut up in ghettos,
sneered at, beaten, enslaved, we always have answered our oppressors with brave singing, dancing, and laughing. Our greatest eloquence, the pith of the joy and sorrow in our unbreakable
hearts, comes when we lift up our faces and talk to God, person
to person. Ours is the truest dignity of man, the dignity of the
undefeated. (Waters 1951, 93)

Ethel Waters's autobiography *His Eye Is on the Sparrow* (1951;
hereafter *His Eye*) is filled with passages like this one, penned
in a testimonial style to which, I'd wager, most Americans
have a sentimental attachment. "Unbreakable hearts," deep but
simple spirituality, and the story of triumph over adversity; the
historical specificity of successive trauma experienced by individuals in various places is sublated—or better, evacuated—in a plea to
recognize the "truest dignity of man." These now-overdetermined
tropes provide history-defying white Americans with a screen
through which to read The Story of Black Americans as one in
which we may identify with Dignity instead of coming to grips

with *our place* in a nation that insistently reinvents forms of en-slavement. I am moved by this story and I want to honor *the will to speak the value of just having survived.* But I want to consider whether white audiences have lost their "ear" for—if we were ever competent to hear—the specificity of Black pain and Black sur-vival. What politics did Waters speak in—or against—in this 1951 autobiography?

Waters writes at the cusp of a cataclysmic era of American civil rights activism, a violent time when crucial ideas about race, identity, and justice were secured *as* civil rights. From our present, post–civil rights vantage point, hers may read as an early, less-politicized relative of the kind of attachment to identity that it is now *passé* to see as naïve. I'm inclined, however, to see in it a richly framed alternative to the concept of Black identity that emerged as the flattened out referent of the citizen who was to utilize civil rights law. Reading Waters today gives us a feel for another affect toward identity than the one that underwrote post–World War II civil rights activism, an affect toward identity resonant with (yet different than) that developed as "identity politics." Indeed, how-ever compelling such identity-expression was, those "minority" activists—women, Blacks, gays—who went through the political transformations of the '60s and '70s and then survived Reagan in the 1980s are now primarily concerned with claiming the social space and economic protections that civil rights laws promised. Few of these architects of identity any longer cling so tenaciously to strict definitions, even of the identity we prefer; most people experience their identifications as multiple, shifting. Many who once asserted identity now talk about the strategic nature of ap-parently essentialist claims. Insistence on reiterating the specific link between a consciousness and a public mark of *being-minority* seems excessive. Perhaps we don't *need* identities in the same way anymore; the decades on the barricades, screaming our names, afforded us some control over our sense of self. Maybe we are just more comfortable with "who we are," or with the invented mem-ory of who we wish we had been.

But I'm reluctant to so quickly assimilate Waters's expression of self to the identity politics now under critique. Dismissing hers as a lesser form of identity politics risks "not hearing" the understanding of race relations she offered her readers and, I'll suggest later, the millions of viewers who saw her in *Pinky*. The well-known slackening of attachment to identity that I just rehearsed rests on the assumption that identities are made and relinquished by collectives and individuals who exercise increasing control over the force of the names applied to them. While comforting, this belief in our ontonominative[1] capacity is self-deluding and, more importantly, politically problematic. The bits and pieces out of which post–World War II minority identities were forged were simultaneously worked out through local political struggles *and* in the imaginary space of popular culture. I am interested in the discourse of identity framed in the problem films, like *Pinky*, that have been the focus of this book. There can be no doubt that it was the countless hundreds of thousands of African Americans and their smaller number of white allies who secured the central logic of minority identity that was crucial to establishing a specific form of claims-making that is characteristic of civil rights law. But this hard-won signal identity was also previewed in the problem films, in both their new Method acting style and their apparently new willingness to expose prejudice in American race relations. The racial construction of audiences, entangled with a material history of segregation in entertainment spaces, makes it possible to argue that Black and white viewers "learned" about emergent racial politics through radically different means. In addition, the expectations—for Blacks and whites—about the *use* of film changed in this period. The several Supreme Court decisions of the early 1950s that effectively ended official film censorship allowed film to represent "political" ideas. "Serious films" were quickly expected to occupy a new place within American political discourse. But while the problem films indicted American race politics, the specific mechanisms of cross-identification entailed by the new genre allowed white viewers to avoid conceding *their* racism—they could embrace the words of the emerging legal discourse of civil rights, recognizing Black people as repositories of rights without recognizing themselves as conduits of structural racism. In the popular problem films, America confessed, and opulently, but refused to testify about its past.

I want to make clear that although I stand among those who wish to question the discourse of authenticity that circulated around the identities we once zealously took up, I am not suggesting that the media invented identities that masses mistook as their true selves. I am searching for something other than the hypodermic model of media effects. Nor do I wish to follow Althusser's (2001/1971) formulation of the media as among the ideologic state apparatuses responsible for "hailing" the body as subject. Both presume that codes operate through mechanisms that are largely transparent to, or at least under the control of, producer-encoders, while the same codes remain opaque to, and are not operated on much by, receptor-bodies. The work of Stuart Hall (1980), Sut Jhally and Justin Lewis (1992), and other inheritors of the Birmingham school has formulated a theory of culture industries that does a good job of replacing these two older analytic positions. However, this work does not quite capture the textual murmurings, and especially their emergence at the threshold of audibility, that I want to examine here.[2] In suggesting that an oppositional identity emerged as a figure in mass media, I do not suppose that a simulacrum identity was copied out longhand by the generation of activists who partook of that media.

Instead, I want to suggest that a new, locally significant Black identity and a publicly consumed companion-body—an object of white photophobia[3]—emerged almost simultaneously, the former through immediate political struggle, the latter as a form of entertainment. As a result, when new racial politics burst into view in national news media, the identity that circulated as the authentic political subject was quickly and easily read by white audiences—already accustomed to a new logic of minority identity worked out in the entertainment medium—*as one and the same*. The sublative logic that made the Black body *sign*[4] racism was transferred onto the representations of "real Black" people engaged in protest. African American activists had produced a new style for their politics, but this was partially reinterpreted by those outside the movement (whites, certainly, but also Blacks who had not been among those explicitly crafting the new Black identities). The autochthonous presentation coincided with the representation available in the "new images" of Blacks that were embodied on film in the 1950s and 1960s by actors like Poitier, Waters, McDaniel, and Edwards, who did not, or not simply, show Black people as they "really are." These new images were worked out simultaneously with the expression and media representation of political Black identities. They were not exclusively a response to Black activists' criticism of Hollywood. These actors, the appearance of a new style in their work (Method, or Method-like), and the kinds of plots and genres in which they appeared suggest that the white audience[5] was being forced to admit that America had oppressed Black Americans long after slavery ended. But to understand this process as a stripping away of ideology, or as an increase in fidelity between image-idea and reality, is to dramatically misconstrue the workings of complex codes like film. Signs are not only conventional but their very means of production is historically contingent. Signs don't sign in the same way; they are individually arbitrary, but their genesis and use are subject to the values and mechanisms of semiogenic domains.[6]

Forging a union between Foucault's historically interested work on discourse and Lyotard's more discerning textual analysis (in *The Differend* [1988/1983]), I want to suggest that marks of identity— Black, gay, Woman—emerged in the 1950s to the 1970s as a special condition of naming. And their special status as nouns that operated cross-referentially between the law, social science, liberation politics, new media, entertainment, and, yes, in the practice of everyday life was not due to a unique relation between such marks and reality or beingness of the oppressed subjectivities that they were thought publicly to indicate. Rather, they invoked a succession of historical situations of wrong that could not—and still cannot—be expressed within the complex of what Foucault might have dubbed American historico-juridical discourses, or what Lyotard calls genres. These names, in Lyotard's formulation, co-present "the universe of the phrase in which they are marked" (Lyotard 1988/1983, 33). The sign-identity that, through local struggle and in popular representation, was stabilized as the referent of civil rights law is not the name of a people subject to historical oppression but a special class of noun: the sign of a *différend* of long duration—a wrong that cannot, yet, find its place in phrasing.

The approach I take here has implications for two politics of representation—self-representation *to* a public and democratic representation *within* the state. By the 1980s, these once-compatible projects found themselves at odds over their interpretation of identity and how it might be used. The possibility of presenting Black oppression to a national public through film, thought to arise in the late 1940s with the decline in film censorship, was less a break in a cultural silence than a reorganization of codes for repressing popular memory of American racism. My argument also hints at means to revivify identities not as claims to being but as a kind of public record of the activities of a society whose most prized historico-juridical discourse protects it from consciousness of its crimes. I want to shift the direction of *this* identity's gaze away from an interior search for a truth of being and reestablish it as a tactical function: to a situated body peering at the multiple possible strategies in a field of power. The structure of the minoritarian identity claim is not that of uncovering a true ontology but of *witnessing* in a situation in which victims are afforded no voice.[7]

The Victim-Witness Story

You are informed that human beings endowed with language were placed in a situation such that none of them is now able to tell about it. Most of them disappeared then, and the survivors rarely speak about it. When they do speak about it, their testimony bears only upon a minute part of this situation. How can you know that the situation itself existed? That it is not the fruit of your informant's imagination? Either the situation did not exist as such. Or else it did exist, in which case your informant's testimony is false, either because he or she should have disappeared, or else because he or she should remain silent, or else because, if he or she does speak, he or she can bear witness only to the particular experience he had, it remaining to be established whether this experience was a component of the situation in question. (Lyotard 1988/1983, 3)

The idea of questioning the accuracy of an apparent victim-witness account of a situation of horror may be unseemly.[8] In passages like this one, Lyotard rubs our noses in just such a debate in order to display the rough logic that undergirds a kind of legal thinking that Western Europe and the United States share as a common legacy (whatever difference existed between French and English law of the modern period, whatever twists the United States has added through refining constitutional democracy). Because he is concerned with ethical judgment not high theory (the density of his writing notwithstanding), Lyotard works through a specific case at the time of his writing: the allegation by far-right French politicians that the Nazi death chambers did not exist.

Haunted by their participation in the events of World War II, or by their parents' participation, torn by continuing revelations about the meaning and extent of collaboration and by the emergence of politicians with fascist pasts and fascist aspirations, Europeans continue to view the Nazi death camps as scenes of ongoing moral crisis. Americans, too, invoke the Nazi death camps as an ultimate test case, but in rather different ways than Europeans. Americans might be revolted by Lyotard's opening because he takes seriously the problem of—and the need for a response to—the claim that the death camps' existence cannot be proved. Americans consider the assertion that the death camps are a hoax to be largely crack-pot, an idea associated with a far right from which, the current toxic levels of nativism notwithstanding, most people would dis-tance themselves. However often "The Holocaust" is invoked by Americans, the referent idea of Nazis and their camps is never-theless tenuous for non-Jewish Americans because we conceive of them as perpetrated by foreigners on another shore. To query the truth of Nazi practice is, for non-Jewish Americans, impolite, but not a moral crisis. The distance between non-Jewish Americans' historical sensibility and Lyotard's, between the conditions of his writing and our reception, complicates discussions of the utility of *le différend* as a concept in contemporary radical thinking.

Let me offer an anecdote. The first time I taught Lyotard's *Differend* (in a graduate rhetorical theory course in 1993–94) I tried to elicit reactions from the students. I sensed they were un-willing to take up the topic of Holocaust history, and so I asked if there might not be other examples of similar collisions between the enormity of an event and the variety of historical representations made of it. As it happened, there were no Jewish-identified students in the seminar, or at any rate, no one spoke on behalf of this subject position. I'm embarrassed to admit that, in the context of the classroom, I failed to challenge the easy distinction between "American" and "European" concerns and memories, which would have so easily been problematized by considering the case of the "Jewish-American." In trying to get a discussion off the ground, I watched the students alternate between silence and hysteria as they tried to produce other cases of le différend. It appeared that in the face of Lyotard's framing example (poor seminar leadership perhaps making the situation worse), they were ashamed to suggest that anything with which they were more closely identified might be grave enough to count as le différend. The very impossibility of incorporating the symbolically European crime into the psyche of American discussions about justice prompted several students, when pressed further, to impulsively offer increasingly extreme but isolated situations with no more reality for them than the massive events of fifty years ago.[9]

I am sure they all believed that the Nazi camps, the stultifying organization of society under the Third Reich, and the ideology of cultural-racial supremacism that underwrote them are unspeakable and that we must be forever vigilant against them. Our concept of Nazi evil, however, seems to have blinded even these sophisticated graduate students to the structured horror of brutalities that are not marked by a name like "Holocaust," or that occur without evident figures of evil as their perpetrators. In the absence of a Hitler (even Saddam Hussein didn't quite make the grade—students were cynical, aware of their potential for anti-Arab racism, savvy about their limited access to accounts of the then-recent and first Bush Gulf War from the "Arab perspective"), we don't quite know what to do about the ethnic bloodbaths in the former Eastern Bloc and in several African states, much less how to come to grips with the role of white Americans in American racism.

It may be that we are only willing to designate such evil persons in retrospect and from the vantage point of a victor's discourse. Had Hitler won, not only would millions more people be dead but we also would not possess any of our discourse of "human rights," historically and culturally contingent on the tenuous possibility of a juridical assembly of nations, operating as they did in the Nuremberg trial. The deeply troubling truth, as Derrida (1986) pointed out in his controversial essay on South Africa, is that current political meta-narratives must continually keep "The Holocaust" and "Apartheid" in view as the ultimate diacritical referent for human rights. We remain *discursively* committed to genocide we oppose in the flesh.

But why not American Slavery?

We white Americans still cannot figure our own history as a slower burning genocide guided by a theory of cultural-racial supremacy that differs only in details and rhetorical style to others that we so easily pronounce evil. "Racism," if I may use shorthand for the locution "theory of cultural-racial supremacy," is still deeply constitutive of American politics and domestic policy. The apparent rise in neo-Nazism and white supremacy in the United States is merely the eruption of a sensibility that is ever present, that we have done more to forget than to eradicate. Before returning to analyze the kind of speech offered in Ethel Waters's autobiography, I want to think along with Lyotard a while longer, keeping in mind the possibility of thinking of American racism—the referent of the indexical dimension of the Black body sign in the problem films—as a *différend*.

Distinguishing Wrongs

Having long abandoned the modernist fantasy of a communicative scene unhampered by interference, Lyotard sets out to frame language use in a way that appreciates power differences and their ethical implications. Lyotard's ethical significance is most easily felt through brief comparison with Richard Rorty's work on irony and contingency (1989).[10] Here, neopragmatism only partially masks a soft version of realism that makes his postfoundationalist ethics more palatable to the Americans who prefer to disdain relativism than come to grips with the consequences of their liberal pluralism. Lyotard's and Rorty's respective engagement with

Wittgenstein (and their different rejuvenation of the idea of language games) gives them a common jumping off point, or rather, affords us a common basis for comparison. But we should not confuse Rorty's guarded relativism with Lyotard's vigilant search for a paralogia[11] that can at least keep us tuned in to the ethical crisis of relative difference.

Both philosophers are concerned with the modalities of language-in-action, but Rorty abandons us in a universe of incommensurable language games; our point of contact comes through translation and persuasion. We can only ever recruit others to our "final vocabulary," Rorty's term for the language-frame any of us settle upon and try to insist that others use.[12] But the intractable nonsecurability of "final vocabularies" raises an ethical issue: how can we know when something inhumane has occurred? Rorty deals with this problem by proposing that we make attempts to win final-vocabulary battles a private philosophical matter, a language game to be conducted with humility and irony. For Rorty, the hard work is to assign private philosophical matters and serious problems of torture and terrorism to separate arenas—a feat he accomplishes by distinguishing between the questions "do you want and believe what I want and believe?" (the liberal ironist's private philosophical game) and "are you in pain?" (the important political question). Rorty attempts to reduce the deleterious effects of heterogeneous language use by reserving one language game, secured through a profound form of subjective transparency—*"are you in pain?"*—for questions of political ethics. This sparest of games is supposed to ensure that we cut through the fundamental rhetoricity of language games in order to find out whether someone has been wronged. The world of speculative philosophizing and persuasion should be entered into ironically, with the recognition that no ultimate truth can be found and that only final vocabularies exist to be argued over and successively replaced. But even after we shift into the pain question game, Rorty does not consider whether we really will *ask the question,* much less whether we will be able to hear a reply. Rorty's citizen is always competent to hear the cry of the oppressed. But haven't decades of political debates and legal decisions about "reverse discrimination" in the United

States made it clear that the key genre designed to make pain cries audible—civil rights law—is unable to distinguish between the various types of cries it hears? The indignant conservative white male sounds "the same" as the Black woman who is—historically and still—locked out of education, jobs, dignity.[13]

Lyotard tries to do something rather different, something *more;* he does not try to reground ethics in a language theory by proposing some mechanism of persuasion and translation—as in the case of "final vocabularies"—or by presuming a fundamental level of intersubjective connection around the *expression* of pain. He admonishes us to acquire a sense of dynamic attention to the conditions of intelligibility for recognizing a wrong. Instead of distinguishing a present case of "are you in pain?"—which inevitably elicits a strange denotative that requires the respondent to violently sever voice and body, that is, "I report that my body is in pain"—Lyotard shifts our ethical attention more forcefully into a reflexive present for which we must take responsibility, that is, *"is it happening?"* Unlike Rorty, who presumes a space in which there is agreement on what pain is and how it should be expressed, Lyotard details the requirements for hearing, for apprehending: the parties to a wrong, the referent or case, and the space of the witness—but without forcing the wronged person to claim his or her pain, or even speak at all, in any predesignated genre.

For Rorty, we are always already amid the chatter of language games; silence marks a suppression of participation. By contrast, Lyotard takes silence seriously as an effect, choice, and tactic. Silence is not being-outside language games, but a symptomatic move in relation to language games or genres. Lyotard suggests that we may have already ruled the pain cry out of the very genres we have designed to remedy harms, for example, ethics or law. The wronged speak to incompetent listeners, may not make sense within designated genres, or may have every reason not to cry out in the first place. But that should not lessen our concern to stay attuned to the reality of a wrong, nor discourage us from experimenting with phrase linkages.[14] Rather than draw lines with respect to final justifications for intervening (this remains a genre), Lyotard considers the dual facet of a wrong. He thus distinguishes between a damage and a wrong *within* the total universe of possible phrase-linkages, a more rhetorically imbued specification of Foucault's (1972) notion of "statement":

> As distinguished from a litigation, a differend *[différend]* would be a case of conflict, between (at least) two parties, that cannot be equitably resolved for lack of a rule of judgment applicable to both arguments. One side's legitimacy does not imply the other's lack of legitimacy. However, applying a single rule of judgment to both in order to settle their differend as though it were merely a litigation would wrong (at least) one of them (and both of them if neither side admits this rule). Damages result from an injury which is inflicted upon the rules of a genre of discourse but which is reparable according to those rules. A wrong results from the fact that the rules of the genre of discourse by which one judges are not those of the judged genre or genres of discourse. . . . The title of this book suggests (through the generic value of the definite article) that a universal rule of judgment between heterogeneous genres is lacking in general. (xi)

For Rorty, there is always an implied judge who can distinguish between liberal ironists' playful debates about serious matters and the cries of those who are in pain. For Lyotard, there is no such Father; judging always lies within genres, not outside them. For Rorty, one may, temporarily, retreat to the comforts of foundationalism to cry, "Foul!" For Lyotard, ethical responsibility resides in our contemplation of the way phrase regimes bind together the referents of names with those authorized to formulate and to hear, and our need to be alert to the possibilities that new phrase linkages may, in unforeseen ways, bring us to witness or hear testimony about new "realities."

This attention to situation shifts away from what I like to characterize as "ethical positivism"; that is, the desire to predict and control political and social results. This modernist belief in the possibility of prediction and control allows those making ethical decisions to disavow the effect of "unintended consequences," viewed as unforeseeable "accidents" rather than *mistakes* that affect real people toward whom the actor has a duty. Instead, Lyotard moves us in the direction of an open-ended paralogia in which the possibility of new links between (but coming from inside) phrase universes always holds open the chance for silences to hold meaning, even to find expression. Thus, Lyotard takes the "reality" of discursivity very seriously without letting particular theories of discourse (which are, finally, limiting "genres") stand in the way of considering that litigation always refuses to hear the heart of the litigant's story. For Lyotard, "are you in pain?" forecloses a phrase universe that might be made present in the act of witnessing, and without any guarantee that the pain represented as "yes" will receive any attention after its constative insertion.

Rorty tries to extract power from the witnessing situation, but by banishing power from the heart of this *event,* by turning it into a perpetually deferrable report because it is always only audible a second later ("are you *still* in pain? still? still . . . ?) Rorty conserves within neopragmatism the indeterminate relativism of which a generation of continental theorists were (incorrectly) accused. How are we to resituate a real "happening" of pain in the supplementary space that Rorty reserves outside philosophical reflection? How can we reflect on the imagined, panoptic metapublic in which the never articulatable universal will exerts its ethical force? For Rorty, the answer is to be found in the classic assertion that pain is absolutely shared, and he reduces ethics to an illusory primordial case: the call to respond to a pain cry. *"But do you feel the same pain I feel?"*

An Ear for the Master's Tropes

> When the girls [of a Lexington, Mississippi orphanage for Black children] sang there was nothing between them and their God. Nothing to stop their voices, rich and full of heart, from reaching Him. These were voices untampered with, and they were raised in song not to impress people or to earn money. They were singing to express something they felt and that they never could say in words if they went to all the Vassars and Howard Universities on earth. (Waters 1951, 231)

If we move past the surface tropes through which we receive this affectively certain narration of the plight of Black folks, we can observe the disjuncture and straining that might suggest the presence of a *différend*. Like the passage that opened this chapter, this episode intimates a sensibility lying on the other side of the one manifest as autobiography—telling one's story—in which an author is required to restrict herself to the words one might learn at esteemed institutions of white women's or Black men's education. The Black woman ... isn't there something she wants to say that cannot be phrased through the writings of white women or Black men?[15]

Waters recognizes herself on the edge of a genre that threatens her status as speaker from the moment she achieves audibility. In her career as a singer and film star, she experimented with direct and indirect means of expressing the wrongs Black women experience. In *His Eye*, she ponders the fate of those expressions when they enter "white time," the space the autobiography was destined to arrive at. It is ironic, though I think not consciously so, that Waters tries in this and a much later autobiography to establish a "true" account of her life, the story of an Ethel beyond the one that was so visible in the dislinked spaces of early- to mid-twentieth-century Black and white popular cultures. Simultaneously the most universal and the most particular expression, the most authentically true and the most deeply suspect account, autobiography is a complicated medium in which to offer up a life. In fact, Waters employs two different autobiographical strategies in *His Eye*: the spiritualist mode of the nineteenth-century slave narrative, in which a single story metonymically illustrates the problems of an entire people; and the Hollywood celebrity "as told to," in which the glamorous and abnormally public "star" is specified, personalized, and individualized.[16]

Waters never manages to conform to, synthesize, or artfully break from either of these highly popular autobiographical modes. Her vacillation between the two ways of writing, between persistent racial trauma and ephemeral stardom, is likely what made the book so unenduring for white audiences. (A writerly note: I had originally ended the sentence with "unenduring." However, many Black auditors and friends asked what I meant. *His Eye* was, I came to realize, an enduring part of their cultural repertoire. In my casual assertion I had replicated precisely the incapacity to "hear" and "imagine" that I am here exploring ... it was happening.) And, perhaps, the conflicts between these autobiographical modes is to blame for the book's striking lack of coherent politics at a pivotal moment in Black civil rights' articulation. At times, the author delights in passing unseen as Ethel Waters. At others, she is annoyed by whites who only perceive a faceless Black type. She tells horrific stories of segregation and discrimination, but then devotes her most sustained emotional passages to her failure as a mother, which she blames on the quest for stardom and her early attraction to the "high life" that critics like Manthia Diawara (1995) have argued was not a disavowal of responsible citizenship but a principle source of Black community aesthetics and politics in the 1930s and 1940s.[17]

In the course of trying out available ways for narrating the truncation of her life relative to her white peers, she employs Black stereotypes that white consumers can be presumed to have easily recognized (though only a few that Black consumers might have held of white ones).[18] Waters drifts toward, but never finds the languages of, Black power, class solidarity, dignified passive resistance, and pan-Africanism—ideas that were vying for centrality in

Figure 15. *Ethel Waters performing the blues.*

postwar Black America's struggle for a political and cultural voice. Indeed, Waters seems to skip a generation of political concepts, jumping over the language of civil rights that would dominate U.S. national antiracist struggles in the decades after the publication of her book. Instead, she voices and sits most comfortably in a centuries' old Black womanism. She links the historical experience of generations of Black women to her own when she describes her stage-acting method in this way: "I was Hagar [a Black female character] that night. Hagar and Momweeze [her mother] and all of us" (247). Simultaneously compressing and embodying Black woman-ness, Waters here constructs an authorial center, an identity, that might seem parallel to the logic of identity that underwrote civil rights law. But where civil rights point to a disembodied essence or consciousness that forms the basis of a class-to-be-protected, Waters speaks an organic unity that can only find performance as an unspoken, even unspeakable figure of what was once called "Soul" behind, and uncontainable in, representations of Black people. I want to consider what Waters's strong formulation of soul was forced to give up when "identity" was required to *represent* Black community in the white political agon of citizenship and rights.

Waters's sense of racial incommensurability and the evasive figure of "Soul" are most articulated when she makes the culturally overdetermined association between "the blues" and Black women's experience. As her story unfolds, we discover that Waters actually does *not* view the blues as a medium through which to communicate Black women's experience to white listeners. On one hand, Waters and her blues are available to the white audience of her performances (as singer, stage actor, film star, and autobiographer); she is simultaneously the Universal Human and a Particular Black/Female. It is, in part, the question of this transposition of experience and yet refusal of comprehension that I am interested in here, because, on the other hand, she persistently complains about how *tedious* white people are; they are outside the blues. She is not worried that she is a poor translator but is, rather, cognizant of the restrictive nature of her genre—its sense, audience, and context. She recounts a conversation with her friend and partner Earl in which he tries to convince her to "translate" the blues:

> The yapping went on, with me insisting white people would be puzzled by my blues, and also bored to death.
>
> Earl argued, "You don't have to sing as you do for colored people, verse after verse after verse of the blues. You can break it up: sing some blues, then talk the story in the song, and end up with more blues. They'll love it." (174)

At this point in *His Eye* Waters rejects the possibility of cultural translation, even though she takes up her position as blues diva in what she calls "white time." Techniques and strategies may make a Black performer more successful in "white time" but such performances have little to do with the phrase universe out of which a blues singer sings. The blues are not a "final vocabulary" waiting for a good persuader to ensure it wider adoption; nor is it simply a "yes" to the white question, "are you in pain?" To imagine blues as a "yes" suggests, first, that whites are trying to find out if there is a wrong, hence, positioning white knowledge of Black pain as—at least publicly—*prior* to the expression of Black pain; and second, that despite the denials of the speaker, pain is *not* universal, or better, that pain's specificity is important—Black pain requires particular expression (here the blues) that is not iterable in white vernacular.

Waters's understanding of how the blues are taken up by Black performers also seems to place her performance theory outside the liberal pragmatism inherited by Rorty. Unlike Rorty, whose ironic players try to persuade others to use their "final vocabulary," Waters outlines a mode of transmission in which successive performers find each other's blues contagious, playable. In one passage, Waters describes her initial disappointment at her discovery that her brother squandered money she had sent for music lessons. But in the end, though he would be unable to get jobs that required sight reading, and less likely to make money as an accompanist in "white time," the lack of ability to read scores was inconsequential because the songs her brother composed "weren't licks and riffs anyone could catch to write down on paper. Yet Pearl and Reggie [Waters's longtime accompanists], once they'd heard them, could play them" (233).

On their surface, such passages easily collapse into a senti-mental primitivism held near and dear by old-fashioned Southern whites, but also comfortable to liberal whites for different reasons. The soul of Black folks should not be written down. Black pain is supposed to be heard in special genres: slave narrative, blues, gospel, rap music. White audiences want to "identify" with Black pain, not by accepting our legacy as wrongdoers, but by virtue of a Universal Experience of Pain, transcribing ourselves into the pseudo-victims of our own crimes, imagining what it "feels like" to be oppressed instead of taking full stock of the desires and pleasure that impel us on our path as oppressors. The demand for Black illiteracy is the foundation of an ethical appropriation that has become a major cultural commodity; whites want signs of overcoming a hard life, but we do not want to become compe-tent hearers of the "reality" of Black pain. Highly skilled at wring-ing pathos from Black expression, whites drag cultural products across this *différend*. Re-situated for white consumption, the blues, projects like *Roots,* even the popular gansta rap and Black urban realist cinema, reduce Black reality to a representation rather than an event,[19] a past rather than a present in which whites are per-petually implicated as racists. The *happening* in this work becomes a "final vocabulary" that whites use but resist comprehending.[20] Always poised on the edge of understanding/not understanding, titillated but always safely on the sound-baffled side of a phrase universe that will indict us, liberal whites forget what we know about our role in the exploitation of Black bodies and Black minds. Paradoxically, avoiding the *happening* of Black pain requires the invention of a cultural genre; the reproduction of Black phrasings as white entertainment hypervocalizes Black pain in order to ren-der it inaudible in "white time."

In the context of this production-erasure of Black persons/ Black experience, Waters shows extreme attentiveness to the dis-tinctiveness of those who lack the means to publicly bear witness to their lives. Waters tells of a homeless woman to whom she sent small money orders.

Some time later, when I got the receipt from one of the money orders, I noticed that the character of the X scrawled on them had changed. I suspicioned that something had happened to the old lady and that someone else was taking the money orders.

I had a friend in New Orleans investigate to see if the old woman was dead. They reported back to me that she had indeed died recently and one of the neighbors had been taking the money orders and signing for her. So it's true that you can identify any person's X, just as you can a full signature. (158–59)

Waters does not conceive of her beneficiary as an anomic minority victim at sea in a hostile dominant society, but as an individual voice within the fabric of community. Waters also recognizes that the a-literate woman's signature will be read in a particular way in "white time"—here, all Xs are the same, the mark of a lack of mark. Thus, a clash of phrase universes: the particular "X" registers in one as a proper noun, but stands in another as a general sign for a mass of unindividuated signatories whose illiteracy means they cannot fully enter the rule of law. "X" marks the spot where a powerful legal system distinguishes among speakers and establishes which competency to read an X/Signature will count in a literate society. The figure of the signature is mirrored in *Pinky*, in which Ethel Waters plays the word-illiterate person reading signs within and outside the Law.

The middle third of *Pinky* finds white matriarch Miss Em (Ethel Barrymore) contemplating her death and working out how to dispose of her property. Anticipating the objections to her plan to give the plantation to Pinky, she writes a will, which she signs while Aunt Dicey is present but not "witnessing." She later asks Dr. Joe to review and take responsibility for her will but, consonant with J. L. Austin's demand for felicity in the performative, he tells her that the act of "witnessing a will" requires that he must actually see her sign. Invoking a hermeneutic much like the one Waters used in the story above, Miss Em discounts her own literacy and refers instead to the *style* of her signing: "You know my signature as well as anyone!" But Dr. Joe insists that to "be legal," his witnessing must refer to the actual event of watching her write her name, and she agrees to sign . . . again.

Miss Em has now rendered her signature twice, once in the intimate phrase universe of moral intention that she shares with Aunt Dicey, who is present but not reading, and then again in the phrase universe that links her Will with the Law—Dr. Joe specifically Witnessing. The last third of the film depicts the court case that ensues once the white cousins object to Miss Em's will. The fact that Em signed twice is asserted by the plaintiffs as evidence of her insanity. The signing encompasses two performatives, two events, that together precisely indicate an order of knowing that cannot be admitted to "white time." But the plaintiffs do not read that signature as a mere repetition, as a signature seconding itself or as a rendering of *a* will as "The Will." Read in "white time," the signature undercuts its own authority and becomes a kind of X that can be admitted as a mark, but not as the sign of a fully competent Willing within the Law. I want to pursue this discourse of literacy and the Law in *Pinky*, looking finally at a scene in which the universe of Black experience momentarily triumphs within "white time."

"White Time"/Black Place

In this reading, Waters's labor in *Pinky* seeks to interweave the Law's demand for literacy and the social order's demand for racial legibility, a theme that loomed large in the autobiographical treatment of her life up through the release of the film. Shot on one of the largest movie sets of the post–World War II era, the film carves out and racializes space through several juxtapositions of public and private, lived in and lived at. "White time" versus Black communal space: the brightly lit store, town square, and courthouse are set against the shantytown, where the swamp dampens the sun and threatens the borders. White domesticity versus Black habitation: the plantation house, shot in exterior and interior, with both white and Black persons seen entering and leaving, is set against Aunt Dicey's and Jake's shacks, encroached upon by the swamp, darkly lit, shot through interiors or as the object of white gaze. Against this dense geography of race, Dicey Johnson (Ethel Waters) figures the continuity in the experience of a Black person passing between these spaces. Pinky (Jeanne Crain), the passing granddaughter, figures the plasticity of identity, as racial signification is experienced as unstable. Unlike the more-often-discussed 1959 version of *Imitation of Life*, where passing is about shuttling across the liminal space between two worlds, *Pinky* considers the significance of place and region in racial hermeneutics.[21] In an acting debacle reminiscent of Fanon's (1965) description of female revolutionaries' *walk*, the sometimes awkward movements Crain is encouraged to make as Pinky suggest that the nature of presence in the Black and white worlds differs. This implied kinesthetic crisis and Pinky's legibility as a Black person—especially white folks' inability to clearly place her—and Dicey Johnson's relation to the written word are juxtaposed as two regimes of reading, organized and enforced as epistemologies of racial difference. Here I want to look at Dicey Johnson's illiteracy as a figure of Black experience in relation to "white time," a labor that Ethel Waters must certainly have slipped into an otherwise unreadable script.

In early scenes we learn that Dicey Johnson depends on others to convey to her knowledge of the written word and its specific form, the Law. But despite the centrality of scenes of her illiteracy, Dicey Johnson never seems to feel—or be—disadvantaged by her lack of access to these genres. Illiteracy is not a source of her oppression, but a device the film uses to trace the edge of her various relations to "white time."[22] Her illiteracy has a dual role in the formal structure of the film: a mechanism to move the plot, and a figure for an order of knowing.[23] It is important to recognize these scenes' participation, in 1949, in a generation of race thinking that was lived before a particular understanding of racism was embodied in civil rights law. The film evokes—and probably traded in—nostalgia for a time when whites did not have to hear or know about the translocal force of Black thought, when they could fantasize Black life as bounded by the edge of the plantation or urban neighborhood. In the early twentieth century, at least in a more concrete sense than today, literacy was the route into a powerful and restrictive domain; to be literate, or to work with the Law through literate intermediaries, was to be in "white time." More clearly here than in Waters's autobiography, civil rights are in "white time" (and the North); that is, necessary, but not fully compatible with the phrase universe of Black pain.

The film's not-yet-civil-rights-movement sensibility is apparent when Pinky returns to the South and meets the local Black doctor, who tries to convince her to stay in the area and practice her nursing "among her people." The young man represents a new—today we might say conservative—politic of Black self-sufficiency, assuming responsibility for the care of Black residents of the area. (We are led throughout the film to understand that Dr. Joe has always cared for Black citizens. As Tom, a doctor of a younger generation asserts, doctors are scientists and not so easily afflicted with racism.) In the end, of course, Pinky stays, but by re-inhabiting the plantation and not as a member of the cosmopolitan "talented tenth" who were finding a new place for themselves in a South struggling with new civil rights laws. Read today, Pinky is Clarence Thomas or Anita Hill or Condoleezza Rice, the victim of a strange semiogenesis within "white time" that has transformed an otherwise passing person[24] into a Black conservative whose race politics are set in relation to the plantation, not to the spatially labile forms of racism that civil rights begins to conceive.

How do these politics get into the film? Despite Waters's glowing remarks about Elia Kazan's directorial style,[25] I'm not sure he could have known what he was doing. Instead, we can retrospectively unearth the film's quite remarkable figuration of the *différend* of being in "white time" because it lies before the consolidation of a Black identity that, however critical and lifesaving for many Black Americans, was also the mechanism through which White America closed the book on a "pain cry" it had grown tired of hearing. The racial sensibility of *Pinky* is smuggled in by Waters and the extremely accomplished Black cast: they are signifyin' in a big way.

There are three crucial moments in the film's discourse about the reading of documents; that is, about conveying legitimacy through the Word as written. The first two serve as bookends, complementary evocations of the racial relations organized around Black illiteracy. In an early scene, Black man-about-town and folk lawyer Jake reads the return address from a letter addressed to Pinky. Laminating the stereotype of Black criminality to the equally

Figure 16. *Pinky meets young Dr. Canady (Kenny Washington) and contemplates her future if she chooses to remain in the South as a Black woman.*

stereotypical parody of Black semiliteracy, the crime of Black literacy is neutralized through a shtick in which Jake craftily picks the letter from Dicey's pocket. She discovers that he has stolen the letter and snatches it from his hand, tossing it into the stove. She is now doubly unable to retrieve the information from its surface scratchings:

JAKE

Well, you boirn'd it up, didn't you? Well that ain't gonna stop nothing. I got a feeling that a fast letter coming like that is like a shadow movin' forward.

DICEY

You think so?

JAKE

Folks is coming. They come treadin' on their shadows. . . . Of course, I can stop 'em. I got his name and address right here. [points to ear] Didn't I tell ya' I work with my brain? I can write a letter back to him.

> Say, I never seen no colored man write like that, with
> two stamps on the letter and his name and address in
> the corner with an MD after. That means doctor.

Jake's structure of knowing is a hybrid of Black oral tradition and white book learning. His literacy allows him to function in "white time," but only as a con man; he knows what to memorize in order to capitalize on the knowledge literacy affords. He can dart into and poach on "white time," then hide its secrets in his head, but the *line* between the forms of knowledge holds fast. Jake's incomplete understanding of white ways results in a slight miscalculation; he signs the faked return telegram "Pinky" instead of Patricia. Although the change is small to Jake (everyone calls her "Pinky," even the legal notice that later appears on the court house wall lists her as "Pinky Johnson, colored"), the mis-signing alarms Tom, who immediately knows that something is wrong—but not why. "Pinky" is a plausible nickname for Patricia. All Tom knows is that there is something he does not know, and he knows *this* because the note signs off with a nickname that does not register for Tom as an intimacy he shares. (In another scene he calls her "Pet." But without access to the continuity script, it is not possible to tell whether he is meant to use the pet name "Pet" or whether he slips out the "a" of the more usual "Pat.") Restricted by the formal white codes of nicknaming, which fairly systematically derive diminutives from the legal name, Tom cannot imagine that this name marks a racial history. Tom can only view Jake's mis-signing as an alarming violation of the rules he knows for self-designation, though he cannot imagine how or why, and he hurries to the South where he will, in his own confused way, temporarily exit "white time."

A later scene also suggests that orality and literacy are partially connected, not as a structure of translation or interpretation but as performance. After Dr. Joe reads aloud the words of the will, Dicey questions him about whether he has accurately read—ventriloquized—the will: "That what the paper say?" Once established as a script, only a proper representative of "white time" can read the part. Dr. Joe encourages the fully literate Pinky to "read for yourself," but Dicey dismisses her verification of the Word. "It

Figure 17. *In* Pinky, *the Black South is personified in Aunt Dicey (Ethel Waters). Here, in her shack, she talks to the Black community's self-styled legal adviser, Jake (Frederick O'Neal). Still from J. Young,* Kazan *(Newmarket Press, 1999).*

say that for a fact, Doc Joe?" as if his reading, rather than Pinky's, has the force of law. This sense of the written word *as* "white time," *as Law*, reappears at the end of the courtroom scene when the presiding Judge Shoreham discounts all the testimony offered by witnesses and declares the paper, as he has read it, to be valid, which carries with it the obligation to act on its terms.

The pivotal moment of illiteracy's inscription in "white time" occurs in the courtroom scene as Dicey is asked to validate Miss Em's signature. Here the audience might have recalled the logic of race relations established as law in *Plessy v. Ferguson* (see chapter 3), which bound Black and white in a pact of segregation in order to avoid the putatively inevitable eruption of violence. *Plessy*, the law of the land at the time of *Pinky*'s release, was not overturned until the *Brown v. Board of Education* decision of 1954. (*Brown* first appeared in 1949, the year of *Pinky*'s release. *Pinky* was censored in 1950, and the two cases sat together on the desks of our highest court judges until the Court mumbled a reversal of *Gelling* in

1952 before finally returning to *Brown*.) *Pinky* does not seem too conservative if we place it in this agon of Black politics of representation. In this context, Waters can then be read as acting out of a sensibility whose power has been sublated—and disembodied—as the sign of Black essence became restricted to the one we know as the referent person of civil rights law. Indeed, the plot of the film hinges on uncertainty about the law; for *Plessy*, the law is only as good as the a priori enforcement capacity of the state (hence, the decision's reliance on the due process clause). Civil rights law attempts to dematerialize—as unlearnable prejudice—the violent impulses that were once presumed to naturally occur in daily life, the rationale for Jim Crow local codes and practices. Underneath the rhetoric of equality, civil rights made civil order a concern at the highest level of the state. Rather than using due process to *restrict* the possibility of race conflict by circumscribing local conflict, *Brown* imposed local and partial martial law and, in several cases in the 1960s, required enforced desegregation by the National Guard acting under the eyes of federal judges.

Pinky represents a time before the Law changed its mind. In the film, Black residents argue that upholding the letter of the law will unleash a primordial force: racist violence. The whites contest the will out of individual greed (in the case of the relatives) and also out of a collective greed that extends from specific property relations to the structured propriety that made any white, however despicable, lord over any Black, however noble, educated, and just. Miss Em's obligation[26] to Pinky recedes in the face of her legal heir's obligation to sustain the symbol of the plantation, even if its real power is now morally and literally decayed, or as Pinky notes: "Slave built, slave run, and rundown ever since." Waters's few minutes on the stand project in relief the intersection of literacy and law, between signifying and testifying.

Mr. Stanley

[speaks softly, leans toward Dicey, elbow on the witness box rail—right—playing with a ring on his hand]

> Go on Aunt Dicey, you were right there in the room when she was writing her will.

Figure 18. *Aunt Dicey "signifyin'" during* Pinky's *court-room scene.*

DICEY

[lethargically]

Yes, suh. I was sitting right there like I always done when my Pinky was out. And Miss Em was still writin' when I left to take the wash uptown, 'cause Judge Walker and some o' dem is mightly particular about when dey gets dey wash. [laughter, gavel] . . .

MR. STANLEY

[looks up at her and backs away, proceeds around to left side of box]

Now, just one more question, Aunt Dicey. [leans in again, looking her in the eye] What makes you think it was her will that Miss Em was writing that day?

DICEY

I know it was, sir.

MR. STANLEY

Well, you see Aunt Dicey, this is a court of law and you're sworn to tell the truth before God. Some of us think this will may have been written at some other time while your granddaughter was present. Did Miss Em tell you she was writing her will?

DICEY

No, suh, Mr. Stanley.

MR. STANLEY

But you could see the paper she was writing on.

DICEY

[nodding]

Yeh, suh, Mr. Stanley.

MR. STANLEY

Well, now, didn't you see enough of it to know what it was?

PINKY (TO JUDGE WALKER)

He's trying to trap her. He knows she can't read and she'll never admit it.

Come on now Aunt Dicey, let's have an answer.

DICEY

[smiling slyly]

You know, suh, as well as I know, that it ain't manners
readin' what ain't meant for you to read

[cuts to Pinky smiling, laughter in the court, gavel].

This crucial scene juxtaposes the Law's demand for literacy with
a form of Black knowing that cannot be admitted into a court of
law. The script gives Pinky the task of verbalizing the trauma that
the lawyer inflicts. But the entire court must also have known of
Dicey's illiteracy, unexceptional as it was. (The possible exception
to this "knowing" is Tom, who is not a competent hearer; having
left the particular, Northern "white time" *he* knows in order to
retrieve his beloved from the space he doubly fails to understand:
Black experience of racial geography and the white attitudes that
define it.) Formally, Pinky's description ensures that white viewers do not misread this important scene. Diegetically, the line expressing her fear for her grandmother's humiliation also marks
her distance from the power of Black vernacular practices. Indeed,
Dicey finally signifies on Mr. Stanley by playing two whites values against each other: the demand for Black illiteracy and the
demand for Black respect for white property, *white space*. She wins,
and the entire court knows it. Dicey finally avoids the humiliation
of having to admit to the open but unspoken knowledge of her
illiteracy and forces Mr. Stanley to violate a higher order; that is,
the "manners" on which the South's plantation system rose and
eventually fell. She subtly reveals that she completely understands
the court's invocation to "tell the truth before God." In avoiding
perjuring herself with regard to how she knows about the will's
Will, Dicey raises the moral quotient of the system that had for
her entire life deprived her of property. In this moment of triumph
she has produced a different phrase universe, one in which she is
the rhetor, and she has forced the lawyer—usually the rhetor *par
excellence*—to stand as a listener. But her victory is brief. The lawyer violently reasserts his and his law's power by screaming at her

and forcing her to admit that Pinky might have intervened in the production of the will at some time when Dicey was not around.

DICEY

[grimly satisfied]

I reckon she could, sir.

MR. STANLEY

[in a rage]

Your witness.

Indeed, she is the defense's witness. Recalling Miss Em's words to Dr. Joe—"you know my signature as well as anyone!"—Dicey knows the plantation owner best of all.[27] Although she cannot read the will, she "knows" her lifelong friend's handwriting. Critically, she wins not because she is admitted to "white time," nor because she beats it at its own game, but because she is, through the black rhetorical strategy called "signifyin'," able to force the Law to play a different game, and one it does not win. I want to underscore what has happened in this scene: Dicey Johnson does not *represent* the texture and truth of Black oppression, and neither does Pinky, who rejects her role as Black crusader, as she was characterized in the "Negro papers from the North" that Tom, ironically enough, brings with him. In her performance of Dicey, Ethel Waters's achievement is to refuse to allow Black presence to be assimilated in "white time." As an actor, she chooses not to *play the scene* through a display of pain and pathos, but by introducing signifyin' as *an acting* of enormous political force. In her signifyin', Waters has Dicey refuse the knowledge game of witnessing. She asserts the Truth of seeing without reading, and Mr. Stanley is unable to reestablish conventional witnessing as the proper form of testimony. The court has no other course than to read the will *as written*.

A Final Word, a Feeling, a Hope

What a debt we owe to the modality for rights claiming that was gifted to the identity movements of the left. The passion, the clarity of vision, the tenacity in trying against all odds, against the threat of violence—and yet, we do not fully understand the price of this very American legacy.

The version of claiming civil rights that became instrumental(ist?) for lesbian and gay identity politics was rightly criticized, and I was among its harshest critics. The first person statement "I am what I am," at least in the face of heteronormative silencing, where one meant "I demand to be recognized as Other," had a special kind of force because it was uttered from a position of disadvantage in relation to those who were privileged by their heterosexuality. Lesbian and gay identity hoped to form an ethical bond across difference, and much coalition work of the 1980s was structured as a kind of parallel recognition of the identity demands made by minority others. But when these claims crossed—when poor Black women, for example, accused gay white men of racism—there were only vertiginous spaces of temporary and partial privilege that had no collective purchase on the larger structures of oppression that differently and differentially affect so many.

When performativity stepped in to replace identity, the situation, while perhaps better for the selves now loosed from the grip of essentialist identity, was worse from the standpoint of collaborative work across difference. The elaboration of performative reiteration has focused too much on the individual actor, rather than on the simultaneously reconstituting social universe necessary to make a performative sensical. Race and class seem to become other or different components of a performativity of self that slips further and further away from any common space of coalition among those oppressed across differing axes of alterity.

Ethel Waters's formulation and practice of reading in "white time" and Lyotard's reformulated and ethically attuned discourse theory call us to attend, in a new way, to the complex spaces of interrelation. Perhaps the geographical dyad of margin makes better sense than the liberal-statistical idea of minority: with margin-aisle (isle)[28] we can begin to imagine ourselves in the scene of an unheard pain, as yet unhearable wrongs . . . there, over to the side, just behind you, now.

APPENDIX
Pinky: *A Synopsis*

Year:	1949
Run time:	102 minutes
Studio:	Twentieth Century–Fox
Producer:	Darryl F. Zanuck
Director:	Elia Kazan
Novel:	*Quality*, by Cid Ricketts Sumner
Screenplay:	Philip Dunne, Dudley Nichols
Cinematography:	Joeseph MacDonald

Cast

Patricia "Pinky" Johnson . . . . Jeanne Crain
Granny/Dicey Johnson . . . . Ethel Waters
Miss Em . . . . Ethel Barrymore
Dr. Thomas Adams . . . . William Lundigan
Dr. Joe McGill . . . . Griff Barnett
Judge Walker . . . . Basil Ruysdael
Jake Walters . . . . Frederick O'Neal

The film opens with a long take of an apparently white woman carrying a suitcase on a dusty road. A train passes her in the distance. She is, we will learn, Patricia "Pinky" Johnson, returning home somewhere in the deep South. She arrives at a shack and addresses the Black woman who is setting out wash. The woman, Dicey Johnson ("Aunt Dicey" or "Granny"), looks at the younger woman, defers, then, realizing it is her granddaughter, greets and hugs Pinky. In their discussions it comes to light that Pinky has returned home because she has fallen in love with a white man. Says Aunt Dicey, knowingly: "Can't tell 'em, can't not tell 'em."

Pinky moves through the white and the Black towns that have formed around a once grand plantation, the mansion of which is still occupied by the elderly, never-married female heir, Miss Em. While the Black townspeople all quickly recognize Pinky as a member of their community ("Pinky, Pinky Johnson who went up north"), most whites—though they finally "recognize" who/what she is—initially perceive her to be white. Many ugly encounters with "prejudice" ensue.

Miss Em falls seriously ill. Aunt Dicey asks Pinky, the only available registered nurse, to attend to the dying woman, who has no money to pay for her services. At first, Pinky refuses, reviling the old woman and the plantation system that has caused her family's poverty. But Aunt Dicey recounts how Miss Em cared for her when she was ill: "Stayed right there in your little room." As a favor to her grandmother, Pinky begrudgingly agrees to serve as nurse. Over the next days, Pinky comes to love the cantankerous old woman. Unknown to Pinky, Miss Em decides to leave her property to Pinky "for the purpose to which she will put it." Miss Em dies, a distant relative contests the will, and a trial ensues.

Meanwhile, Pinky's white doctor boyfriend, Dr. Tom Adams, has arrived from the North. He does not know she is Black and fails to decode contextual clues when Pinky introduces "Aunt Dicey Johnson, my grandmother." She sends him away, but he returns when he discovers the publicity surrounding the trial in the "papers" and the "Negro papers" "up North," the latter of which have constructed Pinky as a folk hero. He waits out the trial, still uncertain why Pinky has stayed: "It's not about the property . . ." Once the will is upheld, Pinky and Tom go to the mansion, where Pinky muses about Miss Em's favorite objects. Tom is convinced Pinky will sell the property and follow him to Denver, where he has been offered a partnership in a new practice. He admits that they cannot return to Boston because "people there will know, or might find out." Instead, they are to go West, where "there will be no more Pinky Johnson." Pinky is tempted by his offer but decides to stay. Miss Em has left her the property for a reason: "You can change your name, Tom, but I wonder if you can change who you really are." Angered, he leaves.

The final scene shows the use to which Pinky has put the property: a hospital and nursery for Black children and for the training of Black nurses. One of the trainees complains affectionately about Aunt Dicey: "She keeps sending us back with the sheets . . . she says they ain't white enough." The final shot is an outdoor close-up of Pinky's face looking heavenward in front of the sign dedicating the clinic to Miss Em.

NOTES

1. American Celluloid

1. Throughout the book I will use the terms "movie" and "film," but not entirely interchangeably. Sometimes I will even apply both terms to the same entity. In general, I use "movie" when I am thinking more in the popular mode and "film" when I mean to invoke an academic or other formal address of the celluloid medium. Thus, *Pinky* is a movie when we watch, but a film when I consider the place it holds in historical, legal, or critical discourse. I—we—are audience and analyst, and sometimes both simultaneously.

2. In his book *Distinction* (1984), Pierre Bourdieu, analyzing cultural taste in France, notes that film became an academically acceptable object there only when those outside the cultural elites became part of the university. Something like this probably happened in the United States when the GI bill allowed huge numbers of World War II veterans to finance a university education that would previously have been out of their reach. With this influx came an interest in new topics and new modes of inquiry.

3. I do not mean that interpretation is not social or that social practices are somehow "material" in a way that interpretive practices are not. Indeed, as my argument unfolds, I will challenge precisely this kind of split between mental and social activity. But for convenience at this early stage, I leave the distinction in its commonsensical form.

4. The war effort brought with it improved employment opportunities for urban Black men and for white women, two groups that "filled in"

on the home front for the white soldiers conscripted for military service. It is also worth noting that the Black men who did serve in the military played more significant roles than they previously had and were, at least in the U.S. Army, in increasingly integrated platoons. After the war, Black workers were displaced and Black veterans were spat upon, attacked, and prevented from exercising their veterans' benefits. In addition to the absolute demographic and economic shifts among Blacks as a whole, the trauma of returning from a modestly improved wartime social world to virulent racism stunned Black leaders and activists for the rest of the decade. It is a commonplace, and one to which I wish to add nuance here, that the 1954 *Brown v. Board of Education* (347 U.S. 483, 1954) decision rejuvenated Black civil rights efforts. It might be true that the publicity surrounding the case placed Black equality in education on the media map. Coverage of *Brown* was not a catalyst but rather emblematic of a larger shift in representing Blackness, a corollary in the print news to the shift I here discuss in film.

5. The problem films start with *Gentleman's Agreement* and *Crossfire*, two 1947 films about anti-Semitism, and extend through *Intruder in the Dust* (1949), *Home of the Brave* (1949), *Lost Boundaries* (1949), *Pinky* (1949), and *Native Son* (1951).

6. Most film commentators maintain that narrative films—of which one subset is melodrama—remain the domain of "chic flicks," while action films are "guy movies." Slasher/horror films confound this truism: as Carol Clover's (1987) ethnographic audience studies of the 1980s suggested, there are routes of cross-gender identification, especially masochistic ones, available in such films. Indeed, in the late 1990s and early 2000s, the wildly received *Charlie's Angels* (2000, 2003) films and their critical doppelganger, the *Kill Bill* movies (2003, 2004), suggest that the feminist survivor latent in earlier slasher film plots has now come out full force in rather violent and nonnarrative feminist revenge films. Nevertheless, the demographic divide still remains, perhaps only because marketing and social practices of interpretation continue to "teach" us to enjoy according to gender.

7. I have given papers on *Pinky* many times over the past decade and a half, and invariably, one or two older members of the audience have offered testimonials about the significance of the film in their lives. Women, and especially Black women, seem indeed to have responded enthusiastically to the film. Several older Black women have described how their extended network of female friends and relatives attended *Pinky* together. While the practice of making movie viewing into an outing was far more common in the 1950s, the fact of such group viewing suggests, as Jacqueline Bobo (1988) showed in the case of *The Color Purple* (1985) thirty years later, that

there was an already-formed Black female audience for *Pinky,* one keenly interested in incorporating their experience of the film into their shared frame of reference. Older white women who have offered recollections of the film don't cite with whom they attended as a significant part of the film's import. In their case, the film seems to remain potent in individual memories, but not so much in a collective one. This may, in turn, be a result of an earlier coalescence (see note 9).

8. The Hays Film Code was adopted by the Motion Picture Producers and Distributors of America on March 31 of that year and subsequently widely applied. See http://www.artsreformation.com/a001/hays-code .html for the full text.

9. Having fought for abolition in the nineteenth century and against lynching of Black men in the early twentieth century, white women already had available a separate racial politic that linked women's issues to racial issues. By the 1940s, mass market women's magazines had provided a narrative vehicle for articulating white women's issues through a liberal politic about racism. Though "tragic" and desexualized, the passing woman ended her story with agency and a job: superficially, the plot has "her" release "him" from an impossible cross-race love, but in the end, she enters the world of morally beneficial work (usually nursing). In the passing woman melodrama there is nothing to impede the white female audience member's identification with the central character, and she can effect a role reversal with the white man: instead of being protected by a white man, she could now protect him by violently withdrawing her (true) love. While the solution is, arguably, somewhat masochistic, what the passing/white woman gave up in sexuality, she gained in moral and economic status.

This was not the first time that dominant—white, patriarchal— society had been confronted by a complex analysis of white women's common interests with African Americans generally. The Grimké sisters' abolitionist writings and lectures popularized one logic of white women's common cause with and responsibility for ending the oppression of slaves and dismantling the system of slavery. Even more pointedly accusatory toward white men, the white women's antilynching campaigns of the two decades before *Pinky*'s release argued directly that white women would not accept that violence against Blacks was done to protect them. But despite these political logics, the late 1930s through 1950s appropriation of the passing woman story to express the social malaise of white women was new, and less coherently political. As white female consumerism and ever-cheaper forms of mass media entertainment conspired to form the white female audience, the potential for a nationally coherent but virtual politic became a reality. White women may well have minimized racial difference in order to introject their own form of geographic displacement and isolation into the passing woman's story.

10. This transfer, in turn, may have enabled Schwarzenegger to win himself the California governorship, capitalizing on an emotional reaction against the recalled Gray Davis. Indeed, in some very perverse way, his "gee whiz, now I'm running for office!" style stood in sharp contrast to George W. Bush's apparent duplicity, the sense that he always knew he would be president, what with his dad and brother looking out for him. The totally fabricated Schwarzenegger seemed far more authentic than Bush Jr. Our ability to read through Schwarzenegger's "bad acting" stands up quite well against Bush Jr.'s apparent conviction that he can simply lie and no one will be the wiser.

11. The sexual secrecy part of this analogy has, until recently, overdetermined the racial secrecy part. This is partly because in the 1980s, many writers in gender studies followed a lead they believed to have been offered by Foucault (1990/1978), in which the central secret of the modern West is sexual, a perversion. The next phase of work (Diggs 1993; Goldsby 1993) made clearer that there are two more-or-less independent discourses of the secret. The other concerns racial categorization understood as a more literal interiority carried in the blood. Although each secrecy narrative is related to a biomedical discourse and, as Foucault (1980/1972) notes in his "Politics of Health in the Eighteenth Century," they arise as a part of the same knowledge–power formation, they are coincident rather than fully mutually constituting. Thus, the relationship between them must not be *assumed* but *demonstrated* case by case.

12. The balance between the apparent conflicting demands for separation of church and state and the free expression of religion that has tipped toward allowing religious groups a greater role in civic life (e.g., through prayers in public and the siphoning of tax dollars to religious-based charities and providers of social services) has a long history, only one interesting chapter of which concerns film censorship. The Catholic Church was enormously influential in detailing the kinds of images and plots that should be proscribed in films, but this was most encoded in the industry's self-policing standards. The vast majority of actual film censorship bodies (most at the municipal level) limited when and where films could be shown, mainly extending "blue laws" based in Puritan beliefs about what could and could not be done on the Sabbath. Thus, Catholics ruled through content, Protestants through zoning.

13. Whatever the problems with *Pinky,* the movie offered a unique vehicle for the expression (however brief) of Black realness and attempted to create a cinematic space for passing. The closure of Method as Universal/ white makes it impossible, by Sirk's *Imitation,* to have "real Blackness"

on film in any of the established mainstream dramatic forms. Critics who laud the performativity of Sirk's *Imitation* are reading a genre whose rules they already accept. In chapter 5 I will return to the question of the possibility of recognition and justice across difference. For now, I raise several historical questions about the validity of the race-gender-sexuality linkage.

14. The background of the Hays Code is discussed in chapter 3.

15. The mulatto character is usually a female—one exception is the passing male doctor/World War II veteran in *Lost Boundaries*.

16. Hays Code 1930, General Principle 1.

17. The urban neorealism of films of the early 1990s rely on this association and, in fact, play on its partial truth: *New Jack City* and *Ricochet* are premised on the authenticity of the musicians-turned-actors who star in the films, rap artists whose prior claim to authenticity in their music undergirds the idea that they are playing someone very much like themselves in these films.

18. HUAC Hearings, July 31, 1958 (U.S. Congress 1958).

19. It is worth recalling the obvious here—that this change takes place less than a century after the American Civil War and barely fifty years after the end of occupation of the conquered South by "American" troops (i.e., Reconstruction, 1863–77). The question of the domestic and the political were actually still quite raw. The subjectivities of Northern and Southern, at least in popular culture, were differently oriented on the question of American identity, racial identity, and racial recognition.

20. On July 29, 1958, a subcommittee of HUAC opened a three-day hearing into communism in the American South. Concerned about not offending the more progressive city of Atlanta, the presiding chairman, Edwin E. Willis of Louisiana (who had taken over duties of the chair of the committee as a whole from Francis E. Walter of Pennsylvania), told reporters: "We are here to trace the web of Communist penetration in the industrialized areas of the South. We picked Atlanta for our hearings because it is centrally located and the gateway to the South. . . . we're not investigating Atlanta as such" (*Atlanta Constitution*, July 29, 1958, 1, 7).

Indeed, while Atlanta's Mayor Hartsfield had welcomed the subcommittee when he learned, earlier in July, that it was headed his way, he commented: "I think there's very little communist activity in this section." Likewise, Georgia Attorney General Eugene Cook offered full cooperation from both his department and the Georgia Bureau of Investigation, although he, too, said there were few communists in the state (Moore, *Atlanta Constitution*, July 11, 1958, 8). As the hearings unfolded, it became clearer that several of those who appeared, notably Carl Braden and Frank Wilkinson, who had appeared before, were preparing another of the several tests of the constitutionality of the committee and its hearings. Thus, threats of privacy violation on the part of the subpoenaed ultimately hampered efforts at information sharing. The extent of the GBI and attorney general's knowledge was at best left vague, a point tersely noted by the *Atlanta Journal* reporter at the end of the hearings: "A congressional investigation with all the trappings has been to Atlanta—flag-waving solons, constitution-waving witnesses, harsh questions, defiant answers. . . . What did it find? So far as Georgia is concerned, the hearings did not produce a single bona fide Communist—or even a Fifth Amendment Communist—now in residence in the state" (Shannon, *Atlanta Journal*, August 3, 1958, 3C).

Shannon described, in only slightly veiled sarcasm, the series of failed efforts to reveal homegrown or even transplanted communists. She chided the subcommittee for suggesting that industrialization, and especially the textile industry, were new to the South. Although she did not openly attack the committee, she presented more favorably than her colleagues at the *Atlanta Constitution* the probability that the hearings were an only thinly veiled attempt to harass white integrationists and Black civil rights activists.

2. In the Hearts of Men

1. The "suspect class" is the law's slip-of-the-tongue attempt to neutrally define a group that it has not yet anointed as a group, one the law has not previously "seen" and "named."

2. This new structure of citizenship would undergo another change in the 1980s when empathy would be fine-tuned into a sense of compassion toward people with AIDS. Ostensibly this should have dampened the negative consequences of discrimination (infected people would thus be persuaded not to "go underground," where they would deprive science of its research object and threaten the mainstream with misrecognized contact). But it must have been a tough love that felt compassion but did not vote in favor of care and education funding measures that might have more equitably distributed health care and more rapidly halted transmission.

3. The legal issues in this period are extremely complex, and the changes occurring in legislation, the courts, the HUAC trials, and in popular culture did not work in concert. The consolidated law regarding how "aliens" might be present in America reveals two fears of invasion: first, that totalitarians would infiltrate and overthrow the government in a bloodless coup (as in, for example, the slightly later *Manchurian Candidate* [1962] and its countless imitators); and second, conversely, that "outsiders" espousing certain social doctrines—especially those concerning

race relations—would use "propaganda" to agitate Americans to destroy each other. Communists would exaggerate racism in favor of world communism, and totalitarians like Nazis would use racial strife to supplant the legitimacy of the American government. Both of these were wistful displacements of the still officially sanctioned separation of Blacks and whites, of course.

Meanwhile, the dislocations of World War II and postwar eras stirred the mix of America's urban melting pots, newly highlighting the cultural diversity of Americans. The increasing mobility of popular culture screened these differences to Americans, suggesting that alternate world views were, within limits, not so threatening. If laws regulating speech had attempted to distinguish between social problems and political issues (the latter uniquely affecting national security because of its contact with a world outside America), the civil rights movement offered a new class of political speech about the social. Because they demanded recognition of a class-based experience, the representatives of those classes, with their "authentic" speech, came to be a sign for a particular political belief. To the extent that this belief was designated political propaganda, that *person* became something like a foreign agent; speech was protected to the extent that a speaker had legitimacy. In the revised Immigration and Nationality Act of 1952 this complex play of status, speech, and advocacy constructs two asymmetrical categories. Thus, being categorized as a communist is performative. Any show of support—giving money or advocating through speech—is treasonous. Pervert status is cast against a grid of already-designated acts of immorality. More explicitly corporeal, it is evidenced through the tracing of past acts (history of incarceration) or through acts or solicitations of outlawed sex.

4. That homosexuals are now considered a class is not largely in dispute. What kind of class and whether they should be added to the list of groups potentially discriminated against is an issue of current debates.

5. One of the remarkable elements of both the 1952 immigration act and *Gentleman's Agreement* is the presumption that the political subject is male. His masculinity may be at stake, but he is, apparently, fully insulated from collapsing into his morphological counterpart. The danger of queerness is not one of collapse into the feminine, but a problem of masculine affect. It would be easy to read queers as the line one crosses between masculine and feminine. But Hobson consistently describes women as having emotions, rather than something I am here calling affectivity.

6. This act reorganized and assembled in one place a range of "laws relating to immigration, naturalization, and nationality; and for other purposes" (163). Most importantly for our purposes here, it revised and altered the use of the 1936 Alien Registration Act, meant to require

agents ("natural" or alien) of alien governments to register their activities. The original intent of this act, an earlier stage for the ambivalence about excluding "foreign" influences while not fully allowing Americans their promised political freedoms, seems to have been to regulate the importation of Nazi propaganda. Thus, this chapter in the drama of American civility is first played out around the figure of the Jew, who is both the object of Nazi propaganda but also, because of the alienness of the Jew/Zionist, considered by the anti-Semite to be a different race. Even the less overtly anti-Semitic viewed Jews as teetering on the brink of allegiance to another nation. Because propaganda connotes foreign ideas, the original law, supposedly protecting the Jew who would become the Zionist, is already full of uncertainty about what constitutes a "foreign" idea. It appears that until the 1960s, "propaganda" applied largely to political ideas proposed by entities other than the U.S. government.

7. Gay civil rights efforts of the 1970s and 1980s and AIDS activism of the late 1980s and 1990s were directed toward removing the sexuality- and health-related sections of this law.

8. There are some notable exceptions: individuals charged with treason or those who were stripped of their citizenship in order to be declared enemy combatants.

9. This partially explains the curious difference in temporality installed between the communist and the pervert or criminal, an ontological difference expressed in the act through specification of a period of time for which the "good moral character" of applicants for permanent residence or naturalization must be demonstrated. Among the violators enumerated in the various sections that cover the morally suspect—stowaways, people who lie about their intentions to eventually apply for naturalization, drug addicts, and people with histories of incarceration—are prostitutes, procurers, and people "coming to the United States to engage in any immoral sexual act" (Sec. 212 [a] [13], 183). Exactly how long one must have been "moral" before entering the United States varies, as does immoralities' alienating capacity should it appear after one gains entry or naturalization. For example, criminality resulting from poverty that has occurred after one's admission is not grounds for deportation. The length of time during which one risked un-naturalization, or alienation, varied; naturalized citizens who acquired communist ideas or affiliations were immediately stripped of citizenship, as were those who in other ways lied to gain admittance. Those involved with sex-related activities had a better chance of beating the charges and retaining their naturalization despite the unnaturalness of their bodily activities.

10. This type of tracking was an FBI obsession begun during Prohibition and is a major means of tracking terrorism today (money laundering

by Arabs, that is, not the economic terrorism of imposed poverty experienced by African Americans.)

11. At this time, the issue of dual citizenship was exhausted by individuals born in a place to parents whose national allegiance was directed elsewhere. The law spells out in some detail the circumstances under which birth does not immediately determine the place of one's "natural" citizenship. With the exception of the American-held territories that lacked statehood, only Canada is mentioned as a sovereign nation whose citizens are not automatically suspicious—technical aliens, but virtual Americans. Soon, natural Americans would be allowed to also hold an Israeli passport. It was not until the 1980s that Americans were widely allowed to hold dual citizenship with any other country: in the midst of renewed right-wing concern about illegal aliens, Irish immigrants filed a suit claiming discrimination because, unlike American-Israeli dual citizens, they could not hold two passports. Subsequently, the U.S. government enumerated a list of countries with which Americans could hold dual citizenship. Of course, these listed countries were viewed as permanent allies, but the policy change also made clearer where the xenophobia expressed as immigration law would be directed.

12. Briefly, Anderson argues that "nation" is a form of imagining a deep political connection, a tie to territory, in the absence of face-to-face contact. The nation sees itself as sovereign, limited, and as a community. What differentiates nations is the way in which they are imagined, not some criterion of true or impostor nationness. For Anderson, the proliferation of print capitalism—a force used by but also autonomous from states—is the medium through which nations have been differentially imagined. In some cases, print capitalism helps produce an official language, while in others, it allows for the stabilization of vernaculars that together form the imagined community of nation. The educational trajectories that allow certain classes of officials to acquire and use the variety of languages and governmental systems cut across the capital interests of media, but also carve out the particular ways in which sovereignty and community are produced as nation. The 1991 revised edition of the original 1983 book takes a slight turn away from the English Marxist spin on Foucault that characterizes this analysis. Anderson examines the role of census, map, and museum in sustaining the sensibility of nation for a given group of people whose affectivity is circumscribed by the iconization of a particular national border.

13. I am here echoing an entire line of research that suggests that modern heterosexuality most clearly emerges when defined against its "other." Thus, the nature and definition of the homosexual, though never stable or complete, emerges in advance of that for "heterosexual." Conceived as

binary, the elements the "two" might hold in common slide back and forth across the line presumed to separate them. However, this line of argument suggests definitions of the heterosexual largely entail being "not that" to articulated definitions of the homosexual. During the reshaping of sexuality that has taken place under the sign of AIDS education, heterosexuality seems to have taken on more solidity and can now "share" practices with homosexuality (for example, anal intercourse); the anatomical configuration of the bodies enables the practice to be marked "heterosexual" and "homosexual" anal intercourse.

14. This understanding of the problem of pluralism's "mind" is discussed in several of the Monique Wittig essays collected as *The Straight Mind* (1992). She never elaborated this critique in a sustained essay and, indeed, neither have I.

15. This subtle shift in emphasis from portrayals of anti-Semitism onscreen toward a focus on "the Negro problem" in film was not unique to Edwards. Ben Maddow, the controversial screenwriter responsible for adapting Faulkner's *Intruder in the Dust* (1949) and a left-leaning man targeted by the HUAC proceedings, also chose to focus on the problem of racism (McGilligan 1989), suggesting a systemic response to growing attacks on "communists" and the anti-Semitic conflation of Jews (and especially Zionists) with anti-Americanism. The move also more squarely places the discourse of conscience in relation to Americans' own domestic history.

16. Obviously, since *Gentleman's Agreement* was released before *Pinky*, it cannot literally "copy" its discourse of passing. But the tropes about passing were already well established for many audiences (see chapter 1, note 9). Hobson published extensively in the women's magazines where these stories had proliferated, and she was influential on, and influenced by, their style and perceptions of audience. That her book became an international bestseller and the subject of an enormously popular film certainly, but only accidentally, helped solidify the interpretive affinity between these different media.

I cite *Pinky* as the sentinel "problem" film about racial passing. Notice the sharp contrast with the more-often discussed film versions of *Imitation of Life,* released before the war (Stahl 1934) and after the problem film cycle (Sirk 1959). Although they are melodramas about women and race relations, their passing character is an example of the racial problematic, not structured as a character of identification for the film's viewers—Black and white, though no doubt with different techne of self-construction. In the *Imitations*, the ineluctably Black and white protagonists carry the audience's principle identification. While providing alternative perspectives on the issue of racial identity, the films do not attempt to teach the viewer how to "walk in the other guy's shoes."

17. See Zelizer 1998 for an example of this trend.

18. Pseudo because the "actuality" of the experience was, in a sense, faked: the reporters believed that they had experienced something very much like the world of the subjects, but only for the period of their immersion. The effect of time and absolute subjective relation to one's own life course cannot be grasped secondhand; for the reverse passer, the narrative time of the Other experience is finite, and the story is told after the fact of the immersion and, hence, ultimately from the place of the teller's nonabsolute subjectivity. The story is necessarily an episode—what it was "like" to be Other for that time, in that place. The hidden universal point of view that enables this snapshot modality of coming to grips with another's reality still plagues liberalist attempts to understand others.

19. As one reviewer put it: "'Pinky' is fooling around with the terrible sickness of bigotry, a mass-market romance given a shot of social responsibility because in the recent past a number of better pictures have shown that it pays to have a conscience" (Hatch 1949).

Indeed, what makes *Pinky* so difficult—both for reviewers then and for viewers today—is this link between a quietist, pre–Second Wave feminism manifest in the "women's film" melodramas and the pointed social critique of the emerging problem film, the other examples of which are war films (*Lost Boundaries, Home of the Brave, Crossfire,* and *All the Young Men,* among others). Where the war films simplistically argue the absurdity of racial distinction in the face of manly bonds, *Pinky*'s version of antiracism juxtaposes the mandates of social cohesion and cultural continuity with the arbitrariness of racial categories and the desire for love. This difference helped to sharply split mainstream reception of the film. Unable to reconcile the complex ways in which gender intersects with race to produce different manifestations of racism and sexism, and bereft of later theories of film as polysemous or available to contradictory "encoding" and "decoding," many reviewers simply split *Pinky,* even arguing that it was two films—one about the "race problem," the other about "a person who learns the meaning of life and who finally sees that her own happiness is not the important thing." Combined with the fact that film viewing in the South in this period was racially segregated (often with different times for Black and white showings), this split in critics' reading of the film suggests that, indeed, there was a dual, or even triple, audience—or better, interpretive community—for the film: the young white women who typically attended two double features per week, white men, and Blacks of both sexes.

20. The wartime work of Phil's fiancée, Kathy, is mentioned in order to express her frustration that the identificatory subtly required for the new kind of war eluded women: "During the shooting war, she worked

herself half sick in factories, sold bonds, accepted all the discomfort of ration books and shortages like a good soldier. But during this covert war for this country's future, this secret war in which antisemitism [sic] is one of the most familiar weapons, she is unable to do more than offer little clucking sounds of disapproval" (228–29).

21. Film viewership figures for the period, along with the wide and cross-class popularity of women's magazines, suggest that women were the major consumers of the product forms in which the "problem" was discussed, but this only tells us the brute demography of the most direct way of consuming these ideas. The last decade or so of research on television soap operas suggests that while women still constitute the major direct audience for these latter-day relatives of film and magazine melodrama, many men, despite their stated disdain of "women's" products, actually consume them, or keep up with their plots through reviews or discussion. The compounding role of presentation of self through media ("I'm the sort of person who reads the *Times*, not the sort who watches daytime TV") means that demographic data does not tell the whole story of who directly or indirectly consumes, how the content and sensibilities presented in gendered or class-structured media circulate, or how discussions occurring within a particular class of media frame individuals' sense of political values.

22. The imaginary space of a multicultural America was already present in the "boy gang" films of the 1930s and the war films of the 1940s and 1950s. Each featured a "real" group with "one of each" ethnicity, marked by performing the stereotyped role that contributed to the whole. War films, for example, gave Black or Native American soldiers a sixth sense to "know" when the enemy was near.

23. This desire for a true account of the other did not die. Novels, film, and television have continually revived the plot of someone who intentionally or unintentionally ends up living out part of their life as an other. In the 1990s, the TV series *Quantum Leap* took this obsession to new heights with a sci-fi show organized around a brilliant, affable scientist who discovers a theory of space-time that allows him and his homo-erotic/panicked holographic friend to "leap" into the lives/bodies of others in order to redo history, sometimes saving individuals' lives for their private benefit, sometimes altering the course of history (the white, married protagonist gets to start the civil rights movement, the women's movement, the gay movement, and save chimps who are being abused by his own agency—NASA). Reality television may herald another change in the calculus of presentation of self and, with it, the assumptions about intersubjectivity that you-are-there formats relied upon. Reality television circumvents the mediation of the self-other relationship by actors, who,

in the Method, serve as a relay. Reality television turns presentation of self into a nasty little affair as interpersonal relationships shift from an opportunity to understand difference to a strategic and temporary relationship en route to "winning." Instead of witnessing the transcendence of socially embedded conflicts like racism or sexism, as in the problem film and subsequent social dramas, reality television gives us the inside track on domestic squabbles, implying that conflict is grounded in the pressures of spending too much time in close proximity, rather than a result of spending too much time in alienated segregation from others.

24. The problem of disqualifying particularities, and ones that are precisely marked as states of victimization, was displayed in relief in the representation of the O. J. Simpson trial. The very inclusion of Black female jurors rendered the criminal trial both "a jury of peers" and one in which impartiality was impossible, since as women and as Black they were apprehensible by the Universal but could only act as particulars. In order to be victims of discrimination, one must be not-the-Universal; that is, a minority or particular. Thus, still today, even in the very moment in which citizen's rights and duties are at play in legal proceedings, minorities and women are not full citizens by virtue of their dual status as jurors and as objects of discrimination (Patton 2003).

25. Anti-Semitism is dangerously demasculinizing for the Jew as well as the country: "But day by day the little thump of insult. Day by day the tapping on the nerves, the delicate assault on the proud stuff of a man's identity. That's how they did it. A week had shown him how they did it" (Hobson 1946, 97).

26. I have wondered why Laura Z. Hobson did not seem concerned with aligning her treatment of the hot-button debates of her time with nascent feminism. Interestingly, she later penned a book that appears to be a barely fictionalized account of a homosexual son, *Consenting Adult* (1975), which I think still stands as one of the best expressions of the issues of and responses to the early gay liberation movement. Her own feminism is much in evidence in this book, as it is in her first autobiography, *Laura Z.: A Life* (1986). But I think this retrospective examination of her omission of women's issues from the "social issues" of the post–World War II era supports my contention that race and religion were the first issues registered as "social problems," and the need to constitute an anticommunism in relation to them was the critical first break in the constitution of a new form of subjectivity appropriate to changes occurring in the postwar era. It is far from easy to imagine how the promotion or particularization of women's issues could have oriented to the monumental task of anticommunism.

27. The book is finally incapable of figuring the citizen outside the

Christian heritage. In sorting out why the image of a tree keeps coming into his mind, Phil unselfconsciously links Christianity with the founding of America. He finds what he is looking for (with the aid of Bartlett's) in the New Testament Book of Matthew: "'Either make the tree good, and his fruit good; or else make the tree corrupt, and his fruit corrupt: for the tree is known by his fruit.' There it was, uncompromising, noble—Jesus addressing the Pharisees. It was the everlasting choice for wholeness and soundness in a man or in a nation. They had known it, the patient stubborn men who for years had argued and written and rephrased and fought over the Constitution and the Bill of Rights" (Hobson 1946, 205). It is also worth noting that the plot occurs in December. Phil's choice of time for passing ruins Christmas for his fiancée.

28. I have pondered whether "everything has changed" since the World Trade Centers were felled on September 11, 2001. Though I will leave comprehensive analysis to others (this is, after all, a book about the late 1940s), in drawing forward through the genealogical lines, I would say that while the language of nationalism has changed to some extent—the word "patriot" no longer draws laughter or connotes Montana militiamen—and while the legislation to effect it was draconian and hastily passed, the structure of nationalistic affect I trace here seems mainly to have found a new object: terrorists instead of communists.

29. Elsewhere (Patton 1996) I have suggested that at least some framings of queerness are incompatible with the liberal pluralism that underwrites lesbian and gay civil rights politics because queerness encompasses a different theory of space, a fundamental category in U.S. law and political theory. However, I also believe that the pressure to make claims comprehensibly political—*to have an agenda*—has caused "queer," as an activist force, to function primarily as a civil rights movement, albeit one that refuses to be clear about what it wants.

3. Censorship and the Problem Films

1. Unlike the film version of *Gentleman's Agreement*, which in my view is quite faithful to the novel, *Pinky* diverges in significant ways from *Quality*, the novel by Cid Ricketts Sumner (1946) on which it is based. The screenplay changes the white doctor ("Chester" in the book and "Tom" in the film) to make him more regionally marked and to lend weight to the development of his character. In the book, we never learn "Chester's" last name; he makes one appearance in the South and is repulsed by the revelation of Pinky's mixed-race heritage. He does not, contra the film, offer to take Pinky away to the West, where no one will know them. Indeed, in the book he does not offer the words that he is

a scientist and doctor and thus able to rise above the petty prejudices around him.

In the book, Frank Canady—the Black doctor from Boston whose role in the film is extremely limited—is given an important scene at the end where he appears (with the suggestion that he is a romantic interest as well as a companion in the quest to bring better health for the locals) to help Pinky make a Black clinic from Miss Em's plantation house. And it is Black journalist Arch Naughton—though represented as wanting to move toward integration too quickly—who stands beside Pinky through her courthouse ordeal. It is white Dr. Joe and not fiancé Chester who receives accolades as the man of learning who sees through race. As the judge says, "Something about the study of medicine gives a man a sane point of view. At least he knows we're all alike, once you cut through the skin" (261). After Pinky inherits the house, the segregationist towns-people, who have tried to lynch Arch Naughton during the verdict reading (the police chief prevents the white men from chasing him out of the building), burn down the plantation house, but not before a number of the Black citizens retrieve the most prized of Miss Em's possessions. This stands in contrast to the scene in the film in which Dr. Tom Adams walks through the house with Pinky and talks about how much the "antiques" will fetch. What's more, the outcome of the fire is treated differently. In the book, the Black hospital is to be founded in the remaining outbuildings, the former slave quarters, rather than in the mansion, where the film locates its future home.

In short, the book, though in many respects reflecting a gradualist approach to racism and a sentimentality toward the nobility or "quality" of educated Blacks, spares Pinky's sexuality by allowing her the love object of Dr. Canady. The book pulls no punches about the intransigence of racism in America, while the film suggests, as was the wont of women's films of the war years, that the heroic female who de-sexualizes herself can conquer all.

Some other details differ as well. The "Mendelian intricacies," the absence of which vexed one film reviewer of the time, are fully elaborated in the book. In fact, there is a suspenseful subplot in the novel in which Pinky tries to get her grandmother to identify her father (and grandfather). Through a "signifyin'" response Pinky long ponders, this thread suggests that male relatives of Miss Em's are the fathers, making Pinky the niece and perhaps half-granddaughter of Miss Em, whose only child died young. The "answer" to this question is finally offered in the trial, when an onlooker blurts out "My Lord, she's the living image of Stevie Pen—" (267). But someone hushes her quickly. We have a strong sense in the book of the duplicity and complexity of the multigenerational rape of Black women—which whites know but are not supposed to speak. The timelessness and generationality of this systematic misuse of Black women's lives is given a time stamp in the book: we know from the first pages that the book is set in 1944–45, and the blurring of the political history—wrought by Arch Naughton, who describes Aunt Dicey as a former slave (her mother was a slave)—is criticized by Pinky as inaccurately portraying the realities of her present-day South. By contrast, we are never given a clear time frame in the film. As the construction of the South (for example, in the Atlanta HUAC hearings—see chapter 1) makes it perpetually backward, this uncertainty about the time frame suggests that we are either "past" the problems represented, or that they persist only in the back reaches of the South. Again, the large role created for the Northern white doctor also suggests that the North has "gotten over" racism, which persists only as a problem in the South.

2. Banned films in the United States in the period in question (1940–59) include *Victory in the West* (1941), *The Outlaw* (1943), *Amok* (1944), *Mom and Dad* (1945), *Curley* (1947), *The Miracle* (1948), *Pinky* (1949), *Wild Weed* (1949), *La Ronde* (1950), *Native Son* (1951), *M* (1951), *Miss Julie* (1951), *Latuko* (1952), *The Moon Is Blue* (1953), *The Gardener of Eden* (1954), *The Man with the Golden Arm* (1955), *Lady Chatterley's Lover* (1955), *Naked Amazon* (1955), *Baby Doll* (1956), *And God Created Woman* (1956), *Don Juan* (1956), *Desire Under the Elms* (1958), *The Lovers* (1958), and *Anatomy of a Murder* (1959).

3. At the time of *Pinky*'s censoring there were seven state censorship boards; one governed only the showing of films on Sundays (Massachusetts), and one had never enforced its censorship laws (Louisiana). There were approximately a hundred cities and towns with local boards. However, it is impossible to know exactly how many existed, since many had been established in the wake of the *Birth of a Nation* controversy but subsequently went unused (Walters 1952).

4. Indeed, sociological work on interracial relationships in this time period (Cayton and Drake 1945) emphasizes the complex differences in gender of the Black versus white partner, as well as the "ethnicity" and immigration status of the white partner and the class of both.

5. Mast (1982) argues that the antimonopoly *Paramount* case of 1947 hinted that the MPPDA's attempts to regulate content was an intellectual form of monopoly, an opening that encouraged litigants to take state censorship cases through to the higher courts. The *Paramount* case was confined to the exhibition, not production, of film, but the court stated matter-of-factly that "We have no doubt that moving pictures, like newspapers and radio, are included in the press whose freedom is guaranteed by the First Amendment" (599). However, as I have noted earlier, the

codes had developed both as a means of avoiding state intervention and as a kind of moral-market testing: striking down state or municipal codes that sought to regulate distribution via content—the only point at which a state agent could act ("prior restraint" was still post-production)—limited the state's potential hold on the industry. The industry applauded the court cases, but continued to try to regulate the content of film in order to avoid extrastate infringement on its product through protest, etc.

6. Although it was finally decided two years later, *Brown* was first heard in 1952, then sent back for clarification of some of the issues.

7. It is important to reiterate that while the two films were censored under very different statutes, the courts treated them as if the laws governing them and the images they contained were equivalent.

8. Frankfurter also submitted brief concurring comments in the *Gelling* reversal that ended *Pinky*'s censoring. He did not, however, avail himself of the opportunity to read and recite reviews of the film as he did in the *Burstyn* judgment. This, despite the fact that, at the appeals level, *Pinky*'s defenders had themselves invoked the magazines *Life* and *Look,* saying that both had run photo spreads about the movie, which the town had allowed to remain on the shelves, without inciting violence. The judge in that case though had scoffed that "apparently the position is that since this was done there is no point in barring the picture" (Criminal Court of Appeals No. 25210).

9. Another small, but not insignificant, difference between *Pinky* and the novel it is based on is that it is Black newspaperman and political activist Arch Naughton and not white Chester (Tom in the movie) who carries the burden of publicizing the plight of Black southerners. In the film, Tom (the space of the new white citizen subjectivity) actually reads the Black newspapers. Thus, the film version not only turns him into a good guy (in the book he is disgusted by Pinky's Blackness), but also attributes to him knowledge of Black struggle and an alternate place ("scientist") from which to enact his nonprejudiced subjectivity. But, as I note in the text, he is not entirely transformed into a figure of support for Black culture, as his solution to the problem of Pinky's mixed racial heritage is to erase it by moving to a place—Denver—where apparently she cannot be "decoded."

10. As I detail in chapter 5, the moral valance of "witnessing" atrocity is uncertain and perhaps, at present, undecidable. How is it possible to sort out voyeuristic consumption of stories or images of victimization from occupying the position of judging-as-wrong the events and sentiments that have led to the acts represented? Indeed, as I have suggested elsewhere (2003), whites get a certain pleasure in "hearing" the N-word; indeed, in saying/not-saying the word indicated by saying the word at

remove. This ambivalence about signifying the racist through the very same words that enact racism is a problematic that arises, at least for mass media, in the semiotic break that occurs in and around the problem films.

11. President Harry Truman's antilynching bill of 1948 made lynching a criminal act.

12. The late '70s were the zenith of pushing the edge of what might be shown where. This was an extension of debates about the nature of cinema occurring in the newly highbrow film criticism world (see Patton 1999).

13. In geometry, a gnomon is the space implied by the regularity of a figure, but left out in an actual representation, a "bite," usually a "miniature" version of the whole, missing from the corner of a rectangle.

4. Acting Up

1. Books like Nella Larsen's *Passing* (1929) center much more on the political and cultural meaning of passing—what it does to the individual, family, and community—than does *Pinky*. In this way, the film is a melodrama about conflicting duties to self and one's people. Interestingly, in this respect *Pinky* is more like current discussions of biraciality: late in the film, Pinky wants to claim herself as both Black and white, a sense of self that Ethel Waters articulates much more strongly as a cultural inheritance in her autobiography. Thus, we have to be careful to separate out each individual artifact dealing with the multiple issues and contexts of racial identity and racial experience.

2. Part of the argument in this volume concerns the ambiguity of racial markings. Other scholars have noted the ways in which white *characters* in film are sometimes very subtly marked—that is, they are presumptively white unless boldly marked not-white, or sometimes hyperwhite through extreme emphasis on indexes of whiteness. But even this important line of argument, as I am taking pains to show here, needs more amplification since racial markings may also serve to govern the entire reading of a film. Thus, marking a body may not always be done for the purposes of characterization.

3. For a good discussion of Peirce, especially regarding the ways his scheme differs from the more widely known work of Ferdinand de Saussure, see Fiske 1982.

4. It is important to note that Peircean semiotics, as opposed to those more commonly in use in literary criticism and derived from Saussure, were always interested in interpretation of the sign; that is, what it means and to whom. While sign-focused, the activity of this semiotic theory was aimed at understanding the relation of social processes and semiotic

processes. Indeed, we can even say that for Peirce, semiotics is a social process. Thus, while signs contain elements that say how to decode a sign, they also intend toward a specific community or audience who will make social sense of its lexical matter. Peirce—and, as I will discuss in chapter 5, Lyotard even more directly—is concerned with mediated interlocution; that is, how signs move through social contexts. Though Peirce's semiotic theory is cumbersome and expansive, his interest in discourse-as-addressed is much closer to J. L. Austin's somewhat later interest in meaning-in-use than to the interest in "langue" developed as a kind of ideology theory by followers of Saussure.

5. Of course this re-raises the question of racism on the stage and in society. The apparent obviousness—the universe of possibilities—of using the Black body in this way results from a culture in which enslaved Blacks were forced to perform emotional labor for whites. This legacy of racialized labor relations vexes antiracist work even still, as antiracist whites nevertheless desire Black comrades to perform the emotional labor of absolution.

6. For Peirce, this set of associations is part of the ground of reception; unlike the most common uses of the Saussurian scheme, the social dimension that forms the basis of reception, and the rules to be applied in "reading" a sign—the lexemic dimension—are understood to be part of the pragmatics of semiology: the sign is a process, not a thing.

7. Such surface racism was offensive but not, in the end, the biggest crime in the overall denial of Black citizenship entailed in the sentimental articulation of "the Negro problem." Critics were correct to point out, though for the wrong reasons, that discussion of "the Negro problem" through melodrama did not take racism seriously. Standpoint and feeling were already feminized and, thus, devalued; critics only carried through on the association when they denied the critical value of melodrama. Absent from their analyses was an understanding of the complex relation America articulates between gender and understanding and between understanding and civic consciousness. As I showed in my discussion of *Gentleman's Agreement,* a form of understanding that might genuinely apprehend personhood across difference was viewed as a kind of queerness.

8. In silent film, Blackness or queerness might have been part of the humor or danger that animated a plot, but they were not so much "in the film" as they were formal compositional elements of the film. In this sense, they did not require acting a part but, rather, referring to meanings that were not easily iconically visualized. Technically speaking, film had difficultly showing a mixed-race or a homosexual person. Lighting and connotative supplements were the only way to help the viewer "to tell" who was "half Black" or gay.

9. I will leave the fleshing out of the argument to others, but it appears to me that "Blaxploitation" films are precisely about contesting this universalistic use of the Black body and Black experience to figure the "race problem." The action orientation of blaxploitation suggested Black agency—both sexual and epistemological—in the face of a Black acting style that rendered Black experience passively available to knowing whites. Think of the difference between Richard Roundtree's Shaft (1971) and Sidney Poitier's Mr. Tibbs (1970); the former is sexy, ruthless, and seeks knowledge, while the latter is attractive, patiently honorable, and already knows.

10. The conditions of production and reception of film Method differed from theatrical Method—even in the same actor—in four ways. First, the camera liberated the actor's body: he or she no longer had to play to the space of the audience, and camera angles and editing ensured that the audience saw the face and the bodily disintegration that had become so crucial in the Method. In this sense, film Method acting could be more subtle and self-contained than stage Method. Second, Method appeared in the context of a specific type of film: the problem film that was defined, at least by the critics, in opposition to the escapism of Hollywood's dream factory ethos. Method was initially used in, and almost immediately came to stand for, seriousness and authenticity, a new willingness to discuss the harsh social realities of life after World War II. It was thus differently received. Third, Method was not explicitly introduced as a theoretical or political intervention, as it had been when introduced into the elite world of theater with its relatively small and reflexive audience. Indeed, popular commentary on the problem film identifies the break as one in genre, not in acting. And finally, movies had an extensive fan structure that was not only nonexistent in theater but was part of marking film as populist. The persistent claim that the fan could not differentiate between the actor and his or her character was distinguished from the theatergoer's ability not only to separate the two but to evaluate various actors' interpretations of famous roles. Method, then, was less a source of new critical evaluation than a potential crisis in fan relations. However, fans quickly accepted the new, semi-oppositional acting style. At least in the case of male stars, being the vehicle of serious social commentary did not diminish sexiness. One might say that by the end of the 1950s, "authenticity" had been eroticized through the dominance of Method-influenced male idols like Marlon Brando and James Dean.

11. The small gap between actor and character was mediated by the gap between audience and actor: fan knowledge confirmed that the actor's gestures matched who the actor "really was." An actor's performance was good if her or his real life did not give lie to the character played.

In classic Hollywood, the audience was interpellated as fans. With the Method, each audience member was expected to introject her or himself into a universal human drama.

12. Reality would reappear in the 1990s on television's ride-along cop shows like *America's Most Wanted* and *Cops* and, to a lesser extent, on the group challenge epics like *Eco Challenge*. These, in turn, gave way, by the new millennium, to *Queer Eye* makeover spinoffs, *Survivor*, and *Fear Factor*. "Reality" settled back into acting with *Desperate Housewives*, the two-decade later sister of David Lynch's *Twin Peaks*. See also chapter 2, note 23.

13. I want to emphasize here that the acting style that looked like Method was also, at least among Black performers, indebted to the work of the precarious Black film companies of the 1920s through the 1940s. These works not only enabled the production of films with themes that were resonant for Black ex-patriots of the Great Migration (who faced new problems in the burgeoning and ethnically complex Northern cities), but encouraged the development of a Black acting form that broke away from the minstrel show style that had been bound up in the negotiations of Southern race relations. The Harlem Renaissance provided one space for the development of a Black modernism that refracted and reappropriated the Orientalizing performance styles that white modernists had developed from African diasporal and Asian forms. While Black drama and film companies, playing to Black audiences under Jim Crow segregation, enjoyed success from the 1930s until the late 1940s—when problem film emerges for Black and white audiences—the budding Black form had little purchase on the proliferating and stultifying "Black acting" (still sometimes performed by whites) of dominant cinema. Not until the 1950s, as the problem film grew in popularity, would this style of acting make its way to Hollywood's carefully built, significantly white, and Northern audiences, and then within the larger shift in film acting I am describing, associated with the introduction of the Method.

14. The Foreign Agents Registration Act of 1936 created a legal definition of propaganda and identified even American nationals as capable of working for foreign countries through distribution of printed material. Film was declared "entertainment" in the *Mutual v. Ohio* or so-called *Birth of a Nation* case of 1915. The meaning of film entertainment is detailed in the New York Board of Censors model code of 1918 and in the 1927 and 1930 codes developed by the film industry.

15. Barrymore had only just come from the New York stage where she had played the lead in *Scarlet Sister Mary*, a major, largely Black production in which Barrymore played in blackface (Hughes and Meltzer 1990).

16. As worthy of its relegation to the dustbin of literary tropes as the

passing story obviously is from a post–civil rights perspective, it can still be seen as a historical step away from its "tragic mulatto" predecessor, which, as many critics have noted, emerged as a useful trope for white authors who could not finally break with white supremacy nor envision utopian solutions to the diagnosed arbitrariness of racial definitions. This figure allowed for a moratorium on critical thinking about racism as such in favor of creating empathy for the apparent "victim" of the failure of racial distinction. *Pinky* and her print cousins challenged this evasion, in part because they had to present the passing figure's whiteness as plausible; they had to tell audiences a story in which love—almost—conquers all. Thus, this particular version of the passing woman read more cohesively as a figure of Black autonomy, over and against—even explicitly—another concept of miscegenation as species degeneration. Unlike the tragic mulatto, who fit in neither of two possible racial landscapes, this new passing woman was caught between two dimensions of the race-gender-class system: the cultural difference of two racially defined worlds and the moral difference between fulfilling family obligation and engaging in meaningful professional work.

5. Two Conversations

1. I use this neologism to refer to a specific process of claiming a name for one's self in which one asserts a link between the self-name and an essential being that has been suppressed or devalued by a dominant naming system. Ontonominativity is meant to imply a theoretical proposition about the power of claiming that the name one has discovered precedes and is more fundamental than the Master's name. The *practice* of ontonominating, then, is bound up in a theory of language that corresponds broadly to Althusser's propositions about interpellation—the name to which you respond is the means through which the ideologic state apparatus asserts its structure of domination. I contest this understanding of the practice and argue instead that these self-namings and the interior qualities of culture and personality they are supposed to index misunderstand as ontological discursive gestures that are actually deontological—questions of ought, of moral duty, that is, these gestures identify the user as someone with a duty toward others similarly situated. This is not, however, a criticism of the names, nor of other naming practices. Indeed, I suggest here that we cannot be sure what is *in* a name that marks the location of a *différend*.

2. In his *Archeology of Knowledge*, Foucault (1982/1972) argues that when a historical epoch is emerging, its characteristic statements are vaguely audible, which he describes as the "first murmurings" of the

new discourse. While Foucault, as a historian, is talking about the rare event of the rupture of one epoch and the formation of another, I find the general idea of fragments that do not yet have their full complement of related discursive elements to be interestingly compatible with the rhetorical theory Lyotard outlines in *The Differend*. The undergirding question of concern of both writers is how sense—in the form of speech acts (Lyotard) or in the form of a power-knowledge relationship—is constituted within specific historical contexts.

3. I am extremely grateful to Dr. Hortense Spillers who, in the question period following my presentation of a different section of this project, reminded me of Fanon's (1967) useful idea of "photophobia." In Fanon's view, the sight of the Black body caused a phobic revulsion for white people. Although I do not entirely accept the psychoanalytic reasoning underlying Fanon's formulation, part of my concern in chapter 3 and its precursor essay, "White Racism/Black Signs: Censorship and Images of Race Relations" (1995b), is how, in the 1950s, the Black body on film ceased to be entirely a trigger of white photophobia and came, instead (or in addition, with certain subgenres), to sign itself as the object of racism. If we think of Peirce's idea of "lexemic" regulation, it might be that the representational Black body can operate in both sign regimes. The question then is how and with what social and political effects the representational (and possibly also the actual) Black body is forced to *mean* for white audiences and white individuals.

4. I mean "sign" as a verb, which I employ instead of "signify" in order to distinguish my use from that of Saussurian semiotics, or Henry Louis Gates Jr.'s (1987) important "play" with "signifyin'." In addition, since this chapter is, in the end, concerned with the law and literacy, I also use "sign" to evoke the quotidian idea of "signing" and "signature."

5. The question of the precise origin of the new style of acting that several Black actors helped to associate with Method in film is complex and underresearched. Certainly there are a number of actors who explicitly worked in the Method or worked with directors associated with the Actors Studio. However, Black actors had long juggled the relation between their "personal experience" and the roles they played, not least in considering whether or how to "adapt" conventions from segregationist white film to independent or Black audience–aimed film. In addition, styles migrated from other art forms—theater most obviously, but also the complex mimicry of minstrelsy and, in the case of Waters, blues. It is likely that while the new style of acting used by key Black actors in 1950s and '60s' "white" Hollywood found a pedagogic and critical language in Method, it actually had much broader roots in a range of other performance discourses and values. Thus, Method is not a single style

but a tendency in the philosophy of acting that eventually gained an audience that treated such performances as a kind of naturalism or display of authenticity.

6. That is, fields from which signs are generated through some, but not a particular or necessary, logic (see Bourdieu 1984 and Peirce 1994).

7. I'm anxious about adopting Lyotard's term "victim" because contemporary American politics and law have very specific uses for it. For example, the problem of the victim-witness is an explicit concern within feminist politics and legal scholarship. When taken through administrative or legal remedies, the rape or harassment victim's history is rendered as evidence both of the crime having been committed and as a possible means of mediating the degree of criminality of the perpetrator. This type of case is an example of *le différend*: a woman's trauma is converted into a public spectacle that forces her to reenact her victimage, thereby entailing a second victimization; this time, in order to show his violation of the law. Once the wrong enters into litigation, the violation of her body and her personhood are displaced in favor of showing the *perpetrator's violation of the law*. Her body is displaced as evidence, no longer even a testament to it own existence.

8. We cast this as "unseemly" because as hearers we are already implicated as perpetrators or as rescuers who failed to respond to a victim. The situation of listening to or dismissing victims is common. Indeed, in U.S. popular culture, at least since the early '50s, racism is figured through presentation of the perpetrator. The Black body invokes the discourse of civil rights, while the figure of the white racist invokes the ambivalent discourse of racial violence. On the other hand, violence against women is more often figured through the scars on the body of the victim. This *différend* between *différends* was mobilized by the defense in *The People of California v. Orenthal J. Simpson;* audibility of one class of victim was privileged over another. Simpson's defense team successfully argued that he had been the victim of a racist police department. Mark Fuhrman operated as the sign of racist perpetrator in relation to Simpson-as-Black-body. I want to argue that because the representation of women's victimization is less codified, Nicole Simpson's body (literally, in the case of the photographs from the death scene) was not admissible as evidence of the crime against her and could not compellingly indict her ex-husband as the "other" in the victim-victimizer dyad. O. J. Simpson could make his claim to be a victim-body by simply being there in the face of Mark Fuhrman. Regardless of who slit her throat, Nicole Brown Simpson was no longer available to testify to the possible motive for her killing.

9. One student wondered how Lyotard's concept of *le différend* "could help" a small child who had been kidnapped, raped, and murdered—an

event reported on the previous night's news. I dubbed this practice—of stopping conversations about complex ethical problems by demanding that abstract concepts (designed for analysis of macro-historical processes) be responsible to sensational micro-events—the "dead baby" logic.

10. In his *Postmodern Condition* (1979) Lyotard uses the case of scientific knowledge development to critique, among other things, Habermas's approach to state legitimation. Drawing his analogy from systems theory, Lyotard argues that we must find a form of legitimation that is based on parology. "Parology must be distinguished from innovation: the latter is under the command of the system, or at least used by it to improve on its efficiency; the former is a move (the importance of which is often not recognized until later) played in the pragmatics of knowledge" (61). He goes on to argue that Habermas assumes that "it is possible for all speakers to come to agreement on which rules or metaprescriptions are universally valid for all language games . . ." and that "the goal of dialogue is consensus. But as I [Lyotard] have shown . . . consensus is only a particular state of discussion, not its end. Its end, on the contrary, is paralogy. . . . A recognition of the heteromorphous nature of language games is a first step in that direction. This obviously implies a renunciation of terror, which assumes that they are isomorphic and tries to make them so. The second step is the principle that any consensus on the rules defining a game and the 'moves' playable within it *must* be local, in other words, agreed on by its present players and subject to eventual cancellation" (65–66).

11. While the term "paralogy" is no longer in Lyotard's technical vocabulary by *The Differend*, the fundamental ideas about the structure of scientific knowledge production and its translation into legal and moral scenarios are present in the analysis. In this way, paralogy and *le différend* are parallel concepts; the first describes the move from universalizing knowledge systems to local ones, and the second describes the situations in which powerful forces attempt to apply universalizing systems but are unable to register the immediate truth that is articulated from outside the rules of the universal system.

12. Rorty is among many Anglo-American philosophers and rhetorical theorists who accept the idea of bounded, linguistically grounded frames. But he, like Kuhn (1970), Quine (1969), Davidson (2001), and, in other European traditions, Habermas (1979) and Gadamer (1981), argues that some process of translation, grounded either in intersubjective or in pragmatic conventions, allows us to reasonably argue that we communicate with each other in a more-or-less power-neutralized way or space. The French poststructural theorists reject this kind of formulation.

13. For my longer discussion of the way civil rights logic in the United

States was disabled by right-wing strategies and activism, see Patton 1993, 1995a, and 1996.

14. Both Rorty and Lyotard use versions of the idea of what the former calls "keeping the conversation going"—that is, preventing ethical decisions from becoming trapped in the game of final (but never Ultimate) vocabularies. For Lyotard, however, this is accomplished through remaining open to the possibility of "linking" silences or speech acts through new logics. In this sense, Lyotard is much less cynical than Rorty; rather than reserve serious ethical matters (pain cries) to a limited and separate domain, however noble, he leaves open the question of what wrongs have been done and how we can make and hear their phrasing.

15. Dozens of edited volumes, monographs, novels, and poetry collections of the last two decades have made this point. For (literary critical) example, Michael Wallace's *Invisibility Blues: From Pop to Theory* (New York: Verso, 1990); *This Bridge Called My Back: Writings by Radical Women of Color,* edited by Cherrie Moraga and Gloria Anzaldua (New York: Kitchen Table, Women of Color Press, 1981); the edited work of G. T. Hull, P. Bell-Scott, and B. Smith, *But Some of Us Were Brave* (New York: The Feminist Press, 1987); and *Reading Black, Reading Feminist: A Critical Anthology,* edited by Henry Louis Gates (New York: Meridian, 1990).

16. Indeed, the Waters's book is co-authored with Charles Samuels, a veteran ghostwriter, but it is impossible to know whether to read this as a sign of the star's lack of a way with words or whether it is an updated version of the authenticating gesture used by abolitionists when they helped produce and circulate slave narratives.

17. The flight from the "high life," figured as a redemption, meant that by the early 1950s Waters renewed her childhood religion and eventually became a performer in the Billy Graham Crusades, a story taken up in her next autobiography, *To Me It's Wonderful* (1972). This work itself employs the format Diawara (1995) identified as a characteristic structure in Black autobiography. He is particularly interested in the *Autobiography of Malcolm X* (1964), the time span of which is roughly the same as Waters's two volumes, although Malcolm X's turn is toward Black nationalism not evangelical Christianity.

18. The literary rationale for, and source of, her characterizations is uncertain, since she was assisted in writing the volume. Waters had a complex theory of white and Black audiences, which must have informed the choices she made. It is also possible that explicit discussions—like the sort she reports with Earl and discusses in the text—also took place with her co-author and publisher. It is useful to recognize that Waters grew up participating in differing racial contexts. In the autobiography,

she describes herself and her experience as comprised of two racial components; one grandmother was white, and Waters traces her desire for culture (undefined—probably meaning "cultivated" and artistic) to this lineage. In her "star" mode operating as a sign of Black artistry, Waters sees herself as a complex product of the same race mixing that *Pinky* tries to explore. Uncomfortably paralleling Jeanne Crain's negotiation of her character's Black grandmother and white benefactrix, Waters says that "I've always thought that I inherited some of the better qualities of both my grandmothers. From little Sally Anderson [Mom], who died in defeat and the grimmest poverty, I got my fighting heart. From Lydia Waters, who died rich but heartbroken and quite possibly tortured by bad conscience, I think I inherited poise, dignity, and whatever intelligence I have" (Waters 1951, 68).

19. It is simultaneously true that such products express genuinely to Black consumers; that is, each product is double—at least. But the gap between the "white time" and its other reinforces rather than breeches the separateness of the genres, in Lyotard's sense. Thus, in understanding reception of works along the racial divide in America, "genre" is *not* the style of a work, but the total context of producer-audience-work-sense. Lyotard's work in *The Differend* has major implications for the long line of research—in which I situate myself—that tries to disengage the repressive from the liberatory aspects of popular culture. The move from production to consumption, from text to reader, still fails to take seriously the ethical problems of mass communication.

20. This dynamic, which is often thought of as "appropriation," continues most strikingly in hip-hop and other generatively Black forms of music today. I would go further than many in my understanding of this situation: Black artists fail to reap full economic benefits of their expressions because, at least for incompetent white ears, the "sound" can always be reproduced. But at the same time, the possibility for white auditors to recognize that "it is happening" in the sounds of Black forms is preempted by disassociating the form from Black presence.

21. Like the many popular renditions of the passing plot—and written in a different way in Nella Larsen's *Passing* (1929)—African Americans can always recognize race, but whites, particularly Northern whites, are easily "fooled" by cultural and physiognomic details. Indeed, Northern white men seem intent on disregarding the marks of Blackness of women whom they love, but always at the price of *making* her *be* white.

22. I want to suggest that the plantation, while it is inhabited by Dicey and Miss Em, is not figured as "white time," even if it is a white space. The pressure to read the relation of the aging women as a spinster couple,

as lesbian, comes from the increasing intimacy of the space in which they spend much of their time; that is, scenes in which the two appear are all in Ms. Em's most intimate domestic space: her bedroom.

23. Interestingly, the structures of literacy/illiteracy play much more in the film than in the novel, perhaps because recognition, misrecognition, and the forms of knowing that contest text require observation of another's *reaction*. While we know what a linguistic description of such matters *means,* this is different than being present in the event of reading/misreading. Thus, if "performativity" is to have any use it must foreground the "event" quality of the performative, à la Lyotard in *The Differend.*

24. I read this diverse triumvirate of highly public Black intellectuals as "passing" in the sense that they rose to their respective positions by largely disavowing the significance of their *race,* even while Thomas, at least, made strategic use of the public charge of racism. As popular media characters, all are positioned as "hoping to succeed," and in this sense, they are closer, as self-made, to "up from slavery" narratives of which Booker T. Washington's so-named autobiography (1901) is only the most famous example. Condoleezza Rice adds an interesting twist; she is the Soviet specialist brought in to transform the "hot war" of terrorism into a "cold war" that forgets the role of the cold war in setting up the very Taliban and later al Qaeda forces it purports to contest. Passing as a cold warrior, Rice and her statesmanship must defy both the plight of Black People in America and their solidarity with people of color across the several monotheistic faiths foisted upon them. We must struggle to read this avowal of terrorism against Lyotard's powerful insistence on the importance of disavowing terror (see note 10 in this chapter).

25. "Elia Kazan came in and replaced [John Ford]. He remade the picture from the beginning. And Kazan, like Guthrie McClintic, had been an actor himself and he understood my problems. Mr. Kazan, God love him, was able to bring out the very best in me. I was able, through his help, to let myself go and live the part of Grannie as I moved before the camera" (Waters 1951, 272).

26. The important duty in the film is, obviously, Miss Em's obligation to repay Pinky for the job she has done in caring for her—a quasi-contractual relationship since Miss Em declares herself penniless when Pinky comes to work. In the novel, however, it is clear that Miss Em is also eager to convey the property to the child of someone who was, very likely, a male relative of Miss Em's. The novel coolly foregrounds Pinky's blood relation to Em: in order to bring their case, the plaintiffs must implicitly deny their kinship to Pinky. In this sense, the novel, for all its sentimentality about race relations, offers a more biting critique of white

Americans, outing the past—and present—expropriation of Black property, Black bodies, and Black minds.

27. Under the terms of the will, Dicey receives Miss Em's clothes and shoes. Apparently, Dicey has always received Miss Em's used clothes. In a baldly Freudian series of lines, she remarks that Miss Em always bought her shoes larger than necessary because, due to Dicey's bunions, Miss Em's shoes would otherwise pinch her feet.

28. I thank my colleagues in Taiwan for this wonderfully homonymic and importantly undecidable English neologism; there was, for a short time at the end of martial law, a left cultural studies journal by the name of *Aisle(Isle)/Margin*. The name both invokes and critiques the use of "marginal" in identity politics and poststructural work.

REFERENCES

Althusser, Louis. 2001. "Ideology and Ideological State Apparatus." In *Lenin and Philosophy and Other Essays*. Translated by Ben Brewster, 127–88. New York and London: Monthly Review Press. First published in 1971 by New Left Books.

Anderson, Benedict. 1991. *Imagined Communities: Reflections on the Origin and Spread of Nationalism*. Rev. ed. London: Verso. First published in 1983 by Verso. Citations are to the 1991 edition.

Austin, J. L. 1975. *How to Do Things with Words (the William James Lectures)*. 2nd ed. Boston: Harvard University Press. First published in 1962. Citations are to 1975 edition.

Bobo, Jacqueline. 1988. *"The Color Purple:* Black Women as Cultural Readers." In *Female Spectators: Looking at Film and Television,* edited by E. Deidre Pribram, 90–109. London: Verso.

Bogle, Donald. 1989. *Toms, Coons, Mulattoes, Mammies, and Bucks: An Interpretive History of Blacks in American Film.* New York: Continuum Books.

Bourdieu, Pierre. 1984. *Distinction: A Social Critique of the Judgement of Taste.* Translated by Richard Nice. Boston: Harvard University Press.

Butler, Judith. 1990. "Performative Acts and Gender Constitution: An Essay in Phenomenology and Feminist Theory." In *Performing Feminisms: Feminist Critical Theory and Theatre,* edited by Sue-Ellen Case, 270–82. Baltimore: Johns Hopkins University Press.

Carby, Hazel. 1985. "'On the Threshold of Woman's Era': Lynching, Empire, and Sexuality in Black Feminist Theory." *Critical Inquiry* 12 (1): 262–77.

———. 1988. "It Jus Be's Dat Way Sometime: The Sexual Politics of Women's Blues, Gender and Discourse." In *Gender and Discourse: The Power of Talk,* edited by Alexandra Dundas Todd and Sue Fisher, 227–42. Norwood, N.J.: Ablex.

Cayton, Horace R., and St. Claire Drake. 1945. *Black Metropolis: A Study of Negro Life in a Northern City.* Chicago: University of Chicago Press.

Clover, Carol. 1987. "Her Body, Himself: Gender in the Slasher Film." *Representations* 20: 187–228.

Commonweal. 1949. "The Screen: Who Is Happy?" (Review of current films, including *Pinky.*) October 14: 15.

Cook, David A. 1981. *A History of Narrative Film.* New York: W.W. Norton.

Courtney, Susan. 2004. *Hollywood Fantasies of Miscegenation: Spectacular Narratives of Gender and Race.* Princeton, N.J.: Princeton University Press.

Cripps, Thomas. 1993a. *Making Movies Black: The Hollywood Message Movie from World War II to the Civil Rights Era.* New York: Oxford University Press.

———. 1993b. *Slow Fade to Black: The Negro in American Film, 1900–1942.* New York: Oxford University Press.

Davidson, Donald. 2001. *Subjective, Intersubjective, Objective.* Oxford: Oxford University Press.

de Certeau, Michel. 1984. *The Practice of Everyday Life.* Translated by Steven Rendall. Berkeley and Los Angeles: University of California Press.

de Grazia, Edward, and Roger Newman. 1982. *Banned Films: Movies, Censors and the First Amendment.* New York: R.R. Bowker Co.

de Lauretis, Teresa. 1984. *Alice Doesn't: Feminism, Semiotics, Cinema.* Bloomington: Indiana University Press.

Deleuze, Gilles. 1986. *Cinema 1: The Movement Image.* Translated by H. Tomlinson and B. Habberjam. London: Anthlone Press.

Derrida, Jacques. 1986. "Racism's Last Word." Translated by Peggy Kamuf. In *Race, Writing, and Difference,* edited by Henry Louis Gates, Jr., 329–38. Chicago: University of Chicago Press.

Diawara, Manthia. 1995. "Malcolm X and Black Public Sphere: Conversionists versus Culturalists." In *The Black Public Sphere: A Public Culture Book,* edited by The Black Public Sphere Collective, 39–52. Chicago: University of Chicago Press.

Diggs, Marylynne. 1993. "Surveying the Intersection: Pathology, Secrecy, and the Discourses of Racial and Sexual Identity." *Journal of Homosexuality* 26 (2/3): 1–19.

Dyer, Richard. 1997. *White*. London: Routledge.

Eco, Umberto. 1984. *Semiotics and the Philosophy of Language*. Bloomington: Indiana University Press.

Fanon, Frantz. 1965. "Algeria Unveiled." In *A Dying Colonialism*, 35–68. New York: Monthly Review Press.

——. 1967. *Black Skin, White Masks*. New York: Grove Press.

Fiske, John. 1982. *Introduction to Communication Studies*. London: Methuen & Co.

Foucault, Michel. 1980. "Politics of Health in the Eighteenth Century." Translated by Colin Gordon et al. In *Power/Knowledge: Selected Interviews and Other Writings, 1972–1977*, edited by Colin Gordon, 166–82. New York: Pantheon. Originally published in English 1972.

——. 1982. *The Archeology of Knowledge*. Translated by A. M. Sheridan Smith. New York: Pantheon. Originally published in English 1972.

——. 1990. *The History of Sexuality: An Introduction*. Translated by Robert Hurley. New York: Vintage Books. Originally published in English 1978.

Gadamer, Hans-George. 1981. *Reason in the Age of Science*. Translated by Frederick G. Lawrence. Cambridge, Mass.: The MIT Press.

Gaines, Jane. 1988. "White Privilege and Looking Relations: Race and Gender in Feminist Film Theory." *Screen* 29(4): 12–27.

Gates, Henry Louis, Jr. 1987. *Figures in Black: Words, Signs, and the "Racial" Self*. New York: Oxford University Press.

Goffman, Erving. 1959. *Presentation of Self in Everyday Life*. New York: Doubleday Anchor Books.

——. 1963. *Stigma: Notes on the Management of Spoiled Identity*. New York: Simon & Schuster.

Goldsby, Jackie. 1993. "Queens of Language: *Paris Is Burning*." In *Queer Looks: Perspectives on Lesbian and Gay Film and Video*, edited by Martha Gever, John Greyson, and Pratibha Parmar, 108–15. New York: Routledge.

Guerrero, Ed. 1993. *Framing Blackness: The African American Image in Film*. Philadelphia: Temple University Press.

Griffin, John Howard. 1962. *Black Like Me*. New York: Penguin Books, Signet Classics Edition.

Habermas, Jürgen. 1979. *Communication and the Evolution of Society*. Boston: Beacon Press.

Hall, Stuart. 1980. "Encoding/Decoding." In *Culture, Media, Language: Working Papers in Cultural Studies, 1972–79*, edited by the Centre for Contemporary Cultural Studies, 128–38. London: Hutchinson.

Halley, Janet. 1993. "The Construction of Heterosexuality." In *Fear of a*

Queer Planet, edited by Michael Warner, 82–104. Minneapolis: University of Minnesota Press.

Hatch, Robert. 1949. Review of *Pinky,* directed by Elia Kazan. *New Republic,* October 3, 173.

Hobson, Laura Z. 1946. *Gentleman's Agreement.* New York: Arbor House.

———. 1975. *Consenting Adult.* New York: Doubleday.

———. 1986. *Laura Z.: A Life.* New York: Donald I. Fine.

Hughes, Langston, and Milton Meltzer. 1990. *Black Magic: A Pictorial History of the African-American in the Performing Arts.* New York: De Capo Press.

Jacobs, Harriet. 2000. *Incidents in the Life of a Slave Girl.* New York: Penguin Books, Signet Classics Edition. Originally published in 1861 by the author.

James, Joy. 1995. "Black Femmes Fatales and Sexual Abuse in Progressive 'White' Cinema: Neil Jordan's *Mona Lisa* and *The Crying Game.*" *Camera Obscura* 36: 33–46.

Jhally, Sut, and Justin Lewis. 1992. *Enlightened Racism: "The Cosby Show," Audiences, and the Myth of the American Dream.* Boulder, Colo.: Westview Press.

Kuhn, Thomas. 1970. *The Structure of Scientific Revolutions.* 2nd ed. Chicago: University of Chicago Press.

Kushner, Tony. 1995. *Angels in America: A Gay Fantasia on National Themes.* New York: Theatre Communications Group.

Larsen, Nella. 1929. *Passing.* New York: Alfred A. Knopf.

Lyotard, Jean-François. 1979. *The Postmodern Condition: A Report on Knowledge.* Translated by Geoff Bennington and Brian Massumi. Minneapolis: University of Minnesota Press. First published in 1979 by Minuit.

———. 1988. *The Differend: Phrases in Dispute.* Translated by Georges Van Den Abbeele. Minneapolis: University of Minnesota Press. First published in 1983 by Minuit. Citations are to the University of Minnesota Press edition.

McCarten, John. 1949. "The Current Cinema: Darryl in the Dear Old Southland," Review of *Pinky,* directed by Elia Kazan. *New Yorker,* October 1.

McGilligan, Patrick. 1989. "Ben Maddow: The Invisible Man." *Sight and Sound* 58 (3): 180–85.

Mast, Gerald, ed. 1982. *The Movies in Our Midst: Documents in the Cultural History of Film in America.* Chicago: University of Chicago Press.

Michael, Paul, ed. 1969. *The American Movies Reference Book: The Sound Era.* Englewood Cliffs, N.J.: Prentice-Hall.

National Board of Review of Motion Pictures. 1950. "The Negro in Films Today." *Films in Review,* February.

Null, Gary. 1975. *Black Hollywood: The Negro in Motion Pictures.* Secaucus, N.J.: The Citadel Press.

Patton, Cindy. 1993. "Tremble Hetero Swine." In *Fear of a Queer Planet: Queer Politics and Social Theory,* edited by Michael Warner, 143–77. Minneapolis: University of Minnesota Press.

———. 1995a. "Refiguring Social Space." In *Social Postmodernism: Beyond Identity Politics,* edited by Linda Nicholson and Steven Seidman, 216–49. Cambridge: Cambridge University Press.

———. 1995b. "White Racism/Black Signs: Censorship and Images of Race Relations." *Journal of Communication Studies* 45 (2): 65–77.

———. 1996. "Queer Space/God's Space: Counting Down to the Apocalypse." *Rethinking Marxism* 9 (2): 1–23.

———. 1999. "How to Do Things with Sound." *Cultural Studies* 13 (3): 466–87.

———. 2003. "An All-White Jury: Judging Citizenship in the Simpson Criminal Trial Verdict." In *The Discourse of Trauma,* edited by Ana Douglass and Thomas A. Vogler, 129–53. New York: Routledge.

Pearson, Roberta. 1992. *Eloquent Gestures: The Transformation of Performance Style in the Griffith Biograph Films.* Berkeley: University of California Press.

Peirce, Charles. 1994. *From Time and Chance to Consciousness: Studies in the Metaphysics of Charles Peirce.* Edited by Richard S. Robin and Edward C. Moore. Oxford: Berg Publishers.

Petty, Miriam J. 2004. "Passing for Horror: Race, Fear, and Elia Kazan's *Pinky.*" *Genders* 40 (see http://www.genders.org/g40/g40_petty .html).

Quine, Willard Van Orman. 1969. *Ontological Relativity and Other Essays.* New York: Columbia University Press.

Reid, Mark. 1993. *Redefining Black Film.* Berkeley: University of California Press.

———. 1997. *PostNegritude Visual and Literary Culture.* Albany: State University of New York Press.

Ricketts Sumner, Cid. 1946. *Quality.* New York: The Bobbs-Merrill Company.

———. 1949. *But the Morning Will Come.* New York: The Bobbs-Merrill Company.

Rogin, Michael. 1992. "Making America Home: Racial Masquerade and Ethnic Assimilation in the Transition to Talking Pictures." *The Journal of American History,* December: 1050–77.

———. 1996a. *Blackface, White Noise: Jewish Immigrants in the Holly-wood Melting Pot*. Berkeley: University of California Press.

————. 1996b. "The Two Declarations of American Independence." *Representations* 55: 13–30.

Rorty, Richard. 1989. *Contingency, Irony, and Solidarity*. Cambridge: Cambridge University Press.

Russo, Vito. 1981. *The Celluloid Closet: Homosexuality in the Movies*. New York: Harper & Row.

Sánchez-Eppler, Karen. 1993. *Touching Liberty: Abolition, Feminism, and the Politics of the Body*. Berkeley: University of California Press.

Sedgwick, Eve Kosofsky. 1985. *Between Men*. New York: Columbia University Press.

———. 1990. *The Epistemology of the Closet*. Berkeley: University of California Press.

———. 1993. "Privilege of Unknowing: Diderot's 'The Nun.'" In *Tendencies*, 23–51. Durham, N.C.: Duke University Press.

———, and Andrew Parker, eds. 1995. *Performance and Performativity*. New York: Routledge.

Spiller, Hortense J. 1987. "Mama's Baby, Papa's Maybe: An American Grammar Book." *Diacritics* 17 (Summer): 65–81.

Time. 1949. "New Picture." December 12.

U.S. Congress. House. 1952. *Immigration and Nationality Act*. Public Law 414: An Act to Revise the Law Relating to Immigration, Naturalization, and Nationality. U.S. Code, Title 8, Chapter 12 § 1101. Washington, D.C., June 26.

———. 1958. Communist Infiltration and Activities in the South. Hearings of the Committee on Un-American Activities. July 29, 30, and 31.

Washington, Booker T. 1901. *Up from Slavery: An Autobiography*. New York: Doubleday.

Waters, Ethel, with Charles Samuels. 1951. *His Eye Is on the Sparrow*. New York: Doubleday.

———. 1972. *To Me It's Wonderful*. New York: Harper & Row.

Walters, Fred. 1952. "The Supreme Court Ruling on *The Miracle* and *Pinky* Gives Censorship a Punch in the Blue Nose." *Theatre Arts*, August: 74–77.

Winnington, Richard. 1976. *Film Criticism and Caricatures 1943–1953*. New York: Barnes and Noble Books.

Wittig, Monique. 1992. *The Straight Mind and Other Essays*. Boston: Beacon Press.

Zelizer, Barbie. 1998. *Remembering to Forget: Holocaust Memory through the Camera's Eye*. Chicago: University of Chicago Press.

FILMOGRAPHY

All the Young Men. Director: Hall Bartlett. Columbia Pictures, 1960.

The Birth of a Nation. Director: D. W. Griffith. David W. Griffith Corporation, 1915.

Broken Blossoms. Director: D. W. Griffith. D.W. Griffith Productions, 1919.

Charlie's Angels. Director: McG. Columbia Pictures Corp., 2000.

Charlie's Angels: Full Throttle. Director: McG. Columbia Pictures Corp., 2003.

Crossfire. Director: Edward Dmytryk. RKO Radio Pictures, 1947.

Gentleman's Agreement. Director: Elia Kazan. Twentieth Century–Fox, 1947.

Home of the Brave. Director: Mark Robson. United Artists, 1949.

Imitation of Life. Director: John Stahl. Universal Pictures, 1934.

Imitation of Life. Director: Douglas Sirk. Universal Pictures, 1959.

In the Heat of the Night. Director: Norman Jewison. United Artists, 1967.

Intruder in the Dust. Director: Clarence Brown. Metro-Goldwyn-Mayer, 1949.

Kill Bill: Vol. 1. Director: Quentin Tarantino. Miramax Films, 2003.

Kill Bill: Vol. 2. Director: Quentin Tarantino. Miramax Films, 2004.

Like a Prayer. Music video. Director: Mary Lambert, 1989.

Lost Boundaries. Director: Alfred L. Werker. Film Classics, 1949.

Louisiana Story. Director: Robert J. Flaherty. Lopert Films Inc., 1948.

New Jack City. Director: Mario Van Peebles. Warner Brothers, 1991.

The Color Purple. Director: Steven Spielberg. Warner Brothers, 1985.

The Love Mart. Director: George Fitzmaurice. First National Pictures, 1927.

The Manchurian Candidate. Director: John Frankenheimer. United Artists, 1962.

The Miracle. Director: Roberto Rossellini (also known as *Ways of Love;* released in Italy as *Il Miracolo,* or *L'Amore*). U.S. distribution by Joseph Burstyn, 1948.

Native Son. Director: Pierre Chenal. Classic Pictures, 1951.

Night Flight. Director: Clarence Brown. Metro-Goldwyn-Mayer, 1933.

Philadelphia. Director: Jonathan Demme. TriStar Pictures, 1993.

Pinky. Director: Elia Kazan. Twentieth Century-Fox, 1949.

Ricochet. Director: Russell Mulcahy. Warner Brothers, 1991.

The Scar of Shame. Director: Frank Peregini. Colored Players Film Corporation, 1927.

Shaft. Director: Gordon Parks. Metro-Goldwyn-Mayer, 1971.

They Call Me MISTER Tibbs! Director: Gordon Douglas. Metro-Goldwyn-Mayer, 1970.

INDEX

abolition, 145n9

Academy Awards, 1, 7, 11, 47

acting: actors, 3, 10, 16, 82, 91–93, 161n8; actors of color, 50, 85–89, 96–98, 103–4, 110–11, 163n13, 165n5; anti-acting, 10, 96, 146n10; Classic style, 14, 93–96, 101, 105–6, 162–63n11; history of, 3–4, 9–11, 13, 14, 46, 84–85, 88, 90–99, 165–66n5; lesbian and gay, 12, 16; Method, the, 3–4, 6, 10, 15, 16–17, 24, 34, 37, 43, 88, 94–99, 101, 105–6, 109, 111, 146n13, 155n23, 162n10, 162–63n11, 163n13, 165n5; and race, 13, 16, 81–86, 88, 90, 94, 96, 98–106, 163n13; and silent film, 84–85, 90–93, 161n8; stage, 15, 85, 91, 93–94, 162n10, 163n15; techniques,

16, 84, 86, 90–91, 93, 95, 106, 162–63n11, 165–66n5. *See also* censorship: race-related; signs: and race

advertising: and market research, 1–2, 144n6, 154n21

affect, 13–14, 108; and acting styles, 10–11, 15, 34, 84, 90–97, 166n5; and liberalism, 5, 84; and nation, 18, 22–23, 26–31, 36, 38, 156n28

Ahern, Maurice L., 92, 100–101, 104–5

Alien Registration Act, 149–50n6

All the Young Men, 153n19

Althusser, Louis, 110, 164n1

Amok, 158n2

Anatomy of a Murder, 158n2

Anderson, Benedict, 28–30, 46, 151n12; *Imagined Communities*, 28

And God Created Woman, 158n2

Angels in America (Kushner), 44
anti-lynching bill, 160n11
anti-lynching campaigns, 145n9
Archeology of Knowledge (Foucault), 164–65n2
Atlanta, 18; and HUAC 147–48n20, 158n1
Atlanta Constitution, 147–48n20
Atlanta Journal, 147–48n20
audience, 2–3, 7; gender aspects, 34, 144n7, 145n9; interpretive practices, 3, 10, 13, 31 32, 50–51, 62–65, 71, 82, 87, 89, 92, 96, 109, 122, 143n3, 160n2, 162–63n11; racial aspects, 8, 51, 84, 87, 89, 104, 108–9, 111, 121, 144–45n7, 152n16, 153n19, 165n3; regional differences, 76, 163n13
Austin, J. L., 8, 161n4, 125
autobiography, 107–9, 120–28, 160n1, 168n17, 168–69n18, 170n24. *See also* Waters, Ethel

Baby Doll, 158n2
Barrymore, Ethel, 47, 83, 101–4, 125, 139, 163n15
Barrymore, Lionel, 103–4
Birth of a Nation, 8, 49–50, 52–56, 58, 67, 71, 85, 98, 158n3, 163n14. *See also Mutual Film Corp. v. Industrial Commission of Ohio*
blackface, 50, 54, 85–89, 90, 93, 98–99, 104, 163n15. *See also* acting: techniques; Barrymore, Ethel
Black Hollywood (Null), 82
Black Like Me (Griffin), 24, 33
Black Panthers, 5
Black women, 107; and agency,

168n15; and denial of agency, 57, 72–75, 99, 101, 157n1; and desire, 73, 99, 101. *See also* violence: against Black Americans
"Blaxploitation," 162n9
blues, 122–24
B-movies, 6, 33
Bobo, Jacqueline, 144n7
Bogle, Donald, 76
Bourdieu, Pierre, 143n2, 166n6
Braden, Carl, 147–48n20
Brando, Marlon, 162n10
Brick Foxhole, The, 32–33
Broken Blossoms, 58
Brown v. Board of Education, 25, 46, 68, 131–32, 144n4, 159n6
Burstyn (Joseph) Inc. v. Wilson, Commissioner of New York, 49, 52, 68–70, 75, 77, 159n8
Bush, George, Sr., 5, 11, 146n10
Bush, George W., Jr., 146n10
Bush, Jeb, 146n10
Butler, Judith, 8–9, 13
But the Morning Will Come, 100

Catholic activism, 49, 59–61, 69, 91. *See also* censorship
Cayton, Horace R., 55, 158n4
censorship, 15, 25, 52–80; of *Birth of a Nation,* 49, 53–56, 158n3; dismantling of legal means, 48–49, 67–80, 84; enforcement, 16, 48–52, 158–59n5; and First Amendment protection, 49, 55, 60–61, 68–70, 158n5; and Fourteenth Amendment protection, 49, 56, 68–69; history of, 2, 14–15, 50–51, 82, 146n12, 149n3; industry self-regulation, 51–52, 56,

59–64, 68–69, 71, 73, 79; legal means of, 50, 52–53, 59, 79–80, 158n3, 159n7; of *The Miracle*, 48–49, 67–80; municipal, 53, 59, 68, 79, 158n3, 158n5; of *Pinky*, 48–49, 52, 67–81, 98, 158n3, 159n8; provisions, 2–3, 7–9, 13, 15, 18, 50, 52, 145n8, 146n12, 158n3; race-related, 7, 12, 15, 49–52, 56–65, 74, 76–77, 84, 106; "sacrilege"-related, 49, 60–65, 68, 76–77, 79; sex-related, 8, 12, 15, 50, 57, 60–65, 73, 76, 99. *See also* prejudice: as a legal category

Charlie's Angels, 144n6

citizenship, 26–27, 116; and Black Americans, 5, 121, 161n7; changing definitions of, 5, 18–19, 23, 30–31, 35–37, 43–45, 50, 148n2; dual, 151n11. *See also* post–World War II period; Rorty, Richard

civil rights: activism, 3–5, 7, 12, 16, 18, 22–24, 43–45, 55, 72, 76, 88, 108–10, 121–22, 136, 144n4, 147–48n20, 156n29; discourse, 12, 36, 71, 108–9, 122, 128, 148n1, 148–49n3, 164n16, 167–68n13; law, 109, 127, 132

class, 5, 13, 39–40, 103, 137, 145n9, 153n20

classic film, 51, 88

Clinton, Bill, 11

Clover, Carol, 144n6

Cohn, Roy, 44

cold war, 11, 19

Colored Players Film Corporation, 95

Color Purple, The, 144n7

Commonweal, 92, 100–101, 104–5

communism, 6, 18, 21–23, 25, 39, 43, 70, 145n9, 147–48n20, 148–49n3

Consenting Adult (Hobson), 155n26

constitutionality, 49, 55–56, 78. *See also* censorship: and First Amendment protection; censorship: and Fourteenth Amendment protection

consumerism, 6

Cook, David, 35

Cook, Eugene, 147n20

Courtney, Susan, 7

Crain, Jeanne, 14, 47, 64–65, 81–83, 98, 101–6, 127, 139

Crossfire, 31–33, 144n5, 153n19

cross-identification. *See* intersubjectivity

Curley, 158n2

Davis, Gray, 146n10

Dean, James, 94, 162n10

de Certeau, Michel, 9

Defense of Marriage Act, 28

de Grazia, Edward, 60, 74

de Lauretis, Teresa, 85–86

Deleuze, Gilles, 85

Derrida, Jacques, 8, 115

Desire Under the Elms, 158n2

Diawara, Manthia, 121, 168n17

différend, le, 111–20, 128, 164n1, 166n7, 166–67n9, 167n11

Differend, The, 111–16, 165n2, 167n11, 169n19, 170n23

Diggs, Marylynne, 146n11

Don Juan, 158n2

Drake, St. Claire, 55, 158n4

due process, 55, 73–74. *See also* censorship; prejudice: as a legal category

Eco, Umberto, 85
Edwards, James, 2, 16, 32, 97–98, 111, 152n15
ethics, 115–19, 137, 167n9, 167n14, 169n19
experience, 82, 165n5; minority, 5, 24, 38, 41–43, 82, 108–11, 155n24

Fanon, Frantz, 127, 165n3
fascism, 149n3, 149–50n6
film: audiences (see audience); Black companies, 162n13; censorship (see censorship); criticism and reviews, 1–3, 7, 10, 15, 50–51, 69–70, 153n19, 159n8, 161n7; early cinema, 15–16; effects, 3, 10, 53–56, 61–67, 71; as entertainment, 49, 54, 60–61, 65, 69, 92, 110, 163n14; genre, 13, 100, 111, 144n6; history, 2, 14, 49–50, 60, 74, 76; lighting, 161n8; perceived dangers of, 48–50, 54–55, 62–65; and social approaches, 1–2, 49–50; sound, 10, 14, 16, 64–65, 85, 91–96; technology, 3, 10, 13–14; theory, 1–2, 143n1; as vehicle for debate, 49, 69–70, 158n5; and violence (see violence: in film). See also "Blaxploitation"; B-movies; classic film; melodrama; "problem films"; slasher films; urban realism; war movies; women's films
Flaherty, Robert J., 75
Ford, John, 7
Foreign Agents Registration Act, 163n14
Foucault, Michel, 12, 22, 26, 30, 111, 118, 141n11, 164–65n2; *Archeology of Knowledge,* 164–65n2

Garden of Eden, The, 158n2
Gates, Henry Louis, Jr., 82–83, 165n4
Gentleman's Agreement, 4, 6–7, 13, 19, 21, 27, 31–33, 35, 37–43, 45–46, 84, 144n5, 149n5, 152n16, 155–56n27, 156n1, 161n7
Georgia Bureau of Investigation, 147–48n20
God Created Woman, And, 158n2
Goffman, Irving, 3, 9
Goldsby, Jackie, 146n11
government and governmentality, 13, 112–13, 167n10; division of church and state, 13, 25, 42, 146n12; domestic, 6, 18, 21, 24, 27, 31, 34, 39; "feminization" of, 18, 36; national security, 18–19, 39–40
Great Migration, the, 163n13
Griffith, D. W., 8, 49, 53–54, 58; rejection of censorship, 53–54. See also Birth of a Nation; Mutual Film Corp. v. Industrial Commission of Ohio
Griffin, John Howard, 24; *Black Like Me,* 24, 33

Habermas, Jürgen, 167n10
Hall, Stuart, 110
Halley, Janet, 22
Hanks, Tom, 16–17
Harlem Renaissance, 163n13
Hartsfield, William, B., 147n20
Hatch, Robert, 82–84, 98, 103–4
Hays Office Film Code, 8, 15–16,

19, 52, 57, 61–65, 69, 71, 75,
79, 145n8, 147n14
hip-hop. *See* rap music
His Eye Is on the Sparrow (Waters),
107, 119–26
Hobson, Laura Z., 21, 33, 37,
45, 149n5, 152n16, 155n26;
Consenting Adult, 155n26;
Laura Z.: A Life, 155n26
Hollywood, 59, 67, 74–75, 82, 85,
91, 94–96, 101, 111, 162n10,
163n11, 163n13, 165n5
Home of the Brave, 2, 31–32, 97–98,
100, 144n5, 153n19
homophile movement, 22, 88, 108,
136, 155n26
homophobia, 22–23, 32–33, 43–44,
66–67, 87–88, 90
Horne, Lena, 82
House Committee on Un-
American Activities
(HUAC), 6, 18–19, 21–23,
25, 39, 43–44, 147–48n20,
148n3, 152n15, 158n1
Hughes, Langston, 163n15
humanism, 3–4, 10, 21, 30–31, 33,
43, 84, 90, 107, 120, 122, 124,
146n13, 162n9, 167n11
human rights, 11–15

identity: authenticity and "realness," 3, 10, 14–15, 82–84,
88, 96, 110, 146n13, 147n17,
162n10; and civil rights, 4,
12, 121–22, 136; essentialism, 9, 11, 15, 30, 83, 108,
132, 137; hegemonic, 5, 11,
17, 30–31, 38, 40, 42–43,
137, 155–56n27; national, 13,
22–23, 43, 71–72, 147n19;
personal, 3, 9–13, 19; racial,
7, 13, 72, 82–83, 108–111,

122, 128, 147n19, 169n21;
self-consciousness and
interiority, 5, 12–13, 85–87,
96–97; social, 3–4, 6, 8–9,
13, 45–46, 90. *See also* Black
women; interiority; race
Imagined Communities (Anderson),
28
Imitation of Life, 4, 13–15, 46, 102,
127, 146–47n13, 152n16
immigration, 50
Immigration and Nationality Act.
See Public Law 414
Incidents in the Life of a Slave Girl
(Jacobs), 73
interiority, 12–13, 31, 34, 85, 97
intersubjectivity, 5–6, 10–12, 15, 24,
31, 34, 38–39, 46, 109, 155n26
In the Heat of the Night, 17
Intruder in the Dust, 152n15

Jacobs, Harriet, 73; *Incidents in the
Life of a Slave Girl*, 73
Jhally, Sut, 110
journalism, 24, 33–34, 37–38, 43,
69, 153n17–18, 158n5

Kazan, Elia, 7, 14, 39, 47, 72, 97,
102, 105, 139, 170n25
Kill Bill, 144n6
King, Martin Luther, Jr., 2
Kiss, The, 65
kissing, 65–67, 77, 81, 98. *See also*
queerness
Kushner, Tony, 44; *Angels in
America*, 44

Lady Chatterley's Lover
(Lawrence), 158n2
language games, 116–17
Larsen, Nella, 160n1, 169n21;
Passing, 160n1, 169n21

Latuko, 158n2

Laura Z.: A life (Hobson), 155n26

Lewis, Justin, 110

liberalism, 71, 75, 103, 115, 123; as affect, 5, 15, 18, 39–40

Like a Prayer, 81

literacy, 130–36

Lost Boundaries, 100, 144n5, 147n15, 153n19

Louisiana Story, 75

Love Mart, The, 89

Lovers, The, 158n2

Lundigen, William, 64–65, 98, 101–6, 139

Lynch, David, 96

Lyotard, Jean-François, 5, 111–19, 137, 161n4, 165n2, 167n10, 168n14, 169n19, 170n23; *The Postmodern Condition*, 167n10. *See also* silence

Maddow, Ben, 152n15

Madonna, 81

Manchurian Candidate, 148n3

Man with the Golden Arm, The, 158n2

Mast, Gerald, 59–60, 76, 158n5

McCarten, John, 83, 99–100

McDaniel, Hattie, 16, 111

McGilligan, Patrick, 152n15

melodrama, 6, 31, 34–35, 81, 86, 97, 106, 145n9, 160n1, 161n7

Meltzer, Milton, 163n15

Miracle, The, 48–49, 67–70, 75, 78–79, 158n2; censorship of, 48–49, 67–80

"miscegenation," 8, 12, 15, 56–59, 62, 98–99, 101, 164n16

Miss Julie, 156n2

mixed-race persons, 12, 15, 46–48, 58–59, 73–74, 83, 147n15, 159n9, 160n1, 161n8, 164n16

Mom and Dad, 158n2

Moon Is Blue, The, 158n2

Motion Picture Producers and Distributors of America, 60–61, 145n8, 158n5

"mulatto." *See* mixed raced persons; passing narratives

Mutual Film Corp v. Industrial Commission of Ohio, 49–50, 52–56, 68, 71, 75, 79, 163n14

Naked Amazon, 158n2

National Association for the Advancement of Colored People (NAACP), 53

National Board of Censorship (National Board of Review), 59–60

Native Son, 67, 144n5, 158n2

Nazi death chambers, 113–14

neoliberalism, 5

New Jack City, 147n17; and urban realism, 124

Newman, Roger, 60, 74

New Republic, The, 83, 98, 103–4. *See also* Hatch, Robert

New Yorker, 82, 99

Night Flight, 93

Null, Gary, 82–83; *Black Hollywood*, 82

obscenity, 49, 76–80

O'Neal, Frederick, 131

Oscars. *See* Academy Awards

otherness. *See* identity: social

Outlaw, The, 158n2

pain, 5, 108, 116–19, 123–24, 128, 137, 167n14. *See also* Lyotard, Jean-François; Rorty, Richard; violence

paralogia, 116, 167n11

Parker, Andrew, 8
particularity. *See* experience
Passing (Larsen), 161n1, 169n21
passing narratives, 7–8, 14, 33,
    45, 47, 77, 79–83, 99, 102–5,
    145–46n9, 146n11, 146n13,
    160n1, 164n16, 170n24
patriotism: and masculinity, 11, 19,
    38–40
Patton, Cindy, 23, 155n24, 156n29,
    160n12, 168n13
Pearson, Roberta, 84
Peck, Gregory, 33, 35, 37
Peirce, Charles, 13, 85–87, 160n3,
    160–61n4, 165n3, 166n6. *See
    also* signs
performance studies, 9–11, 123
performance theory, 123
performativity. *See* speech act
    theory
Petty, Miriam, 7
Philadelphia, 16–17
photophobia, 110, 165n3
phrase universe, 111, 117–20, 126,
    135
Pinky, 6–7, 14–15, 19, 31, 35,
    37, 46–49, 51–52, 64–65,
    67–68, 71–75, 77, 79, 81–84,
    89–90, 94, 97–106, 109,
    125–36, 139–41, 143n1, 144n5,
    145–46n7, 146n9, 146n13,
    152n16, 153n19, 156n1,
    158n2–3, 159n8–9, 160n1,
    164n16; differences from
    original novel, 75, 156–57n1,
    159n9, 170–71n26; geog-
    raphy, 47–48, 72, 82, 89,
    102–5, 135–36, 158n1, 159n9;
    plot, 47–48, 72–73, 75, 83,
    98, 106; reception, 81–83,
    97–101, 103–05, 109; time
    setting, 82, 89. *See also*

Commonweal; race: racial
    geography
Plessy v. Ferguson, 55, 57, 69,
    85, 131–32. *See also* racism:
    segregation
Poitier, Sidney, 4, 16–17, 111,
    162n9
popular media, 6, 8, 12, 15, 21, 24,
    31, 36, 53, 69, 83–84, 144n4,
    145n9, 151n12, 152n16, 154n21,
    154n23, 159n8, 168n15
pornography, 79
Postmodern Condition, The
    (Lyotard), 167n10
post–World War II period, 1, 12,
    18, 50, 76, 84, 89, 109; and
    changes in the university, 1,
    31, 33, 35, 143n2; and effects
    on women, 35–36, 153n20.
    See also civil rights: activism
prejudice, 50–51, 71–72, 75, 88,
    90, 100, 105, 159n9; as a
    legal category, 8, 48, 54–57,
    68, 71, 73, 75–76, 79, 85,
    98–99, 131. *See also* racism
Privilege of Unknowing (Sedgwick),
    105
"problem films," 3–4, 6, 10, 12–13,
    15, 52, 71, 76, 79, 97, 106,
    109, 144n5, 161n7, 162n10,
    163n13
Public Law 414, 14, 25–26, 149n3,
    149n5, 149–50n6, 150n7,
    150n9

Quality (Sumner), 75, 100, 139,
    156–58n1
Quantum Leap, 38, 41, 154n23
Queer Nation, 44–45
queerness, 9, 12, 16, 22–23,
    25–26, 42–43, 65–67, 90,
    93, 156n29, 161n7–8

race, 11, 70, 127, 164n16; de-
    racialization, 8; interracial
    love, 47–48, 79, 100, 105,
    158n4; relations and "the
    race problem," 4, 13, 24, 40,
    51, 53, 55–59, 73–75, 78, 90,
    109, 155n23, 163n13; racial
    geography, 135–36, 169n22.
    See also identity: racial; *Pinky:*
    geography
racism, 7, 32–33, 35, 50–52, 70,
    87–89, 106, 114–15, 121,
    164n16; anti-Semitism, 18,
    22–24, 32–33, 35–37, 39, 42,
    76, 144n5, 150n6, 152n15,
    155n25; Black experience of,
    5, 14, 24, 28, 51, 56, 70–71,
    73, 99, 148–9n3; in the film
    industry, 4, 7, 56–65, 85;
    and hate speech, 71–80, 103,
    159–60n10; and Jim Crow,
    85, 103, 132, 163n13; and the
    law, 49, 54–57, 127, 166n8;
    in minstrelsy, 84, 93; in the
    post–World War II period, 4,
    10, 18, 143–44n4; segrega-
    tion, 18, 52, 55–56, 59, 79,
    85, 109, 121, 131, 163n13; and
    stereotypes, 4, 7, 22, 53, 81,
    87–88, 90, 101, 103, 121,
    128–29, 154n22; and the U.S.
    South, 52–53, 76, 84, 100. *See
    also* prejudice; signs: and race
rap music, 6, 124, 147n17, 169n20
Reagan, Ronald, 5, 11
reality television, 154–55n23, 163n12
red scare, 25, 40
Ricochet, 147n17
Ronde, La, 158n2
Rorty, Richard, 115–19, 123,
    167n12, 168n14
Rosenberg, Ethel and Julius, 25

Rossellini, Roberto, 48, 78. *See
    also Miracle, The*
Roundtree, Richard, 162n9
Russo, Vito, 15–16, 66

Saussure, Ferdinand de, 160n3,
    160–61n4, 161n6, 165n4
Scar of Shame, 95
school desegregation. *See Brown v.
    Board of Education*
Schwarzenegger, Arnold, 10–11,
    96, 146n10
Sedgwick, Eve Kosovsky, 8, 38, 105;
    Privilege of Unknowing, 105
selfhood. *See* identity
September 11, 2001, 156n28
"sexual perversion," 12, 15, 19,
    26–27, 60, 62, 65, 146n11,
    149n3, 156n9
Shaft, 162n9
Showboat, 100
"signifyin'," 128, 132, 135–36, 157n1,
    165n4
signs, 13, 50–53, 62–65, 78–79,
    85–88, 90, 98, 100, 106, 108,
    111, 160–61n4, 161n6, 165n4;
    decoding 51–52, 86, 161n4;
    genealogy, 51–52; icons, 62,
    66, 74–75, 78–79, 85, 87,
    98, 106, 161n8; indexicality,
    15–16, 50, 62, 66, 75, 78,
    85–87, 89; and race, 8, 10–12,
    50, 52, 60, 73–75, 78–79,
    83–87, 89, 104, 106, 108, 110,
    132, 160n2, 161n8, 165n3,
    169n21; semiotics, 5–6, 15,
    50, 52, 70, 85, 88, 110–11, 127,
    160n3, 160–61n4, 165n3,
    165n4; and sexuality, 10, 12,
    50, 60, 87–88, 161n8; split,
    50–51; symbols, 62, 66, 78,
    85–86; unstable, 12

silence, 117–19, 122. *See also* Lyotard, Jean-François
Simpson, O. J.: criminal trial, 155n24, 166n8
Sirk, Douglas, 4, 13–15, 46, 146–47n13, 152n16
slasher films, 144n6
social geographies, 126–28
"soul" as identity, 122
speech act theory, 8–9, 11, 13, 96, 137, 147n13, 149n3, 165n2, 170n23
Spiller, Hortense, 165n3
Stahl, John M., 14, 152n16
Straight Mind, The (Wittig), 152n14
subjectivity, 50, 106, 120–22, 159n9. *See also* citizenship; identity; intersubjectivity
Sumner, Cid Ricketts, 75, 100, 139, 156n1; *Quality*, 75, 100, 139, 156–58n1

Texas Court of Appeals, 48, 71, 98
They Call Me MISTER Tibbs!, 162n9; Poitier, Sidney, 4, 16–17, 111, 162n9
To Me It's Wonderful (Waters), 168n17

universalism. *See* humanism
urban realism, 124, 147n17
U.S. Supreme Court, 7, 15, 46, 48–49, 51–56, 60–61, 67–71, 75, 79, 84, 109, 131. *See also* censorship: legal means of

Victory in the West, 158n2
violence, 114, 166–67n9; against Black Americans, 4–5, 8, 15, 24, 48, 50, 72–75, 99, 111, 124, 132, 144n4, 145n9; in film, 2, 63–64, 76, 144n6;

incitement to, 48–50, 54–57, 59, 63–64, 71, 85, 98, 131; rape, 57–58, 73–74, 77, 79, 101, 157n1, 166n7, 166n9; trauma, 107, 120. *See also* prejudice: as a legal category

Walter, Francis, E., 147n20
Walters, Fred, 67, 158n3
war movies, 6, 11, 154n22
Washington, Kenny, 129
Waters, Ethel, 5, 7, 13, 16, 47, 83, 88, 98, 101–4, 107–8, 111, 119–37, 139, 160n1, 168n16, 168n17, 168–69n18; *His Eye Is on the Sparrow*, 107, 119–26; *To Me It's Wonderful*, 168n17
Wayne, John, 11
Westerns, 57–58
white supremacism, 8, 86, 100, 114, 164n16
"white time," 120, 123, 125–28, 130–31, 135, 137, 169n19, 169n22. *See also Pinky*
Wild Weed, 158n2
Wilkinson, Frank, 147–48n20
Willis, Edwin E, 147n20
Wilson, Woodrow, 53
Winnington, Richard, 32, 47
Winters v. New York, 69
witnessing, 112, 118–19, 125, 136, 159n10, 166n7
Wittig, Monique, 152n14; *The Straight Mind*, 152n14
W. L. Gelling v. State of Texas, 49, 52, 56, 131–32, 159n8
women's films, 157n1. *See also* melodrama

Zanuck, Darryl F., 100
Zeliger, Barbie, 153n17
Zionism, 43, 150n6, 162n15

CINDY PATTON holds the Canada Research Chair in Community Culture and Health at Simon Fraser University in British Columbia, where she is professor of women's studies and sociology. An AIDS activist and community organizer throughout the 1980s, she is also the author of *Globalizing AIDS* (Minnesota, 2002).